A MINSTERWORTH MISCELLANY

A COLLECTION OF HISTORICAL REAL-LIFE HUMAN TALES FROM A SEVERN-SIDE VILLAGE

St Peter's Parish Church Minsterworth, as seen from across the River Severn.

By
Terry Moore-Scott

Published by
The Minsterworth Community History Project
Lyn Paddock, The Street Minsterworth
Glos GL2 8JJ
Tel: 01452 750160

Researched and Written
by
Terry Moore-Scott

Copyright © 2012

ISBN 13 978-0-9554410-1-1

ISBN 10 0-9554410-1-3

Front cover:

High spring tide on the bank of the River Severn at
The Naight, Minsterworth (Anthony Lynch)

Net proceeds from the sale of this book will go towards
the maintenance of St Peter's Parish Church Minsterworth

FOREWORD

In his book *A History of Minsterworth* (Reardon Publishing, 2006), Terry Moore-Scott gave us an excellent account of the development of this Severnside village 'From Prehistory to 1900'. Thoroughly researched and lacking nothing in detail, yet presenting local history with a light touch, Moore-Scott achieved his objective perfectly. This is an account of a village community, evolving over time that undoubtedly succeeds in enabling the reader to 'appreciate how [Minsterworth] came to be as it is today and, in the process, gain a stronger sense of place and belonging'.

Now, in *A Minsterworth Miscellany*, a worthy addition to that earlier volume, Moore-Scott focuses the lens of his research on selected topics in more intimate detail, ranging historically from the distant past to the modern era. These include an account of the rare medieval Minsterworth Embroidery, now on display in the parish church; fascinating details about village folk, from local gentry to 'Hellfire Jack', a once-famous jockey; the distinguished poet F.W. Harvey (1888-1957); and the inspiring story of Bert Prosser (1903-1997), 'a good all round man', a master craftsman of the type indispensable to every small community at a time when the wheelwright and the cartwright flourished.

It was F.W. Harvey who, in several fine poems, placed Minsterworth firmly upon the literary map. To him the village was the 'Queen of riverside places' whose 'sweet shape of land and winding river' was set for ever in his heart. Terry Moore-Scott, in his two chronicles, places Minsterworth distinctively upon the local history map: a microcosm of the English village.

© 2011 Anthony Boden

CONTENTS

	Page
Sketch map of Minsterworth parish	1
I. Victorian Minsterworth	2
II. The House that Daniel built	18
III. Just a Piece of Old Cloth	29
IV. Lamentable Happenings	42
V. Hellfire Jack	49
VI. Why should the Devil have all the Best Songs	56
VII. Going, Going, Gone...	69
VIII. Literary Links	81
IX. 'A Good All Round Man': the Life and Work of Bert Prosser	96
Bibliography and Author's Acknowledgements	106
Index of contents	110

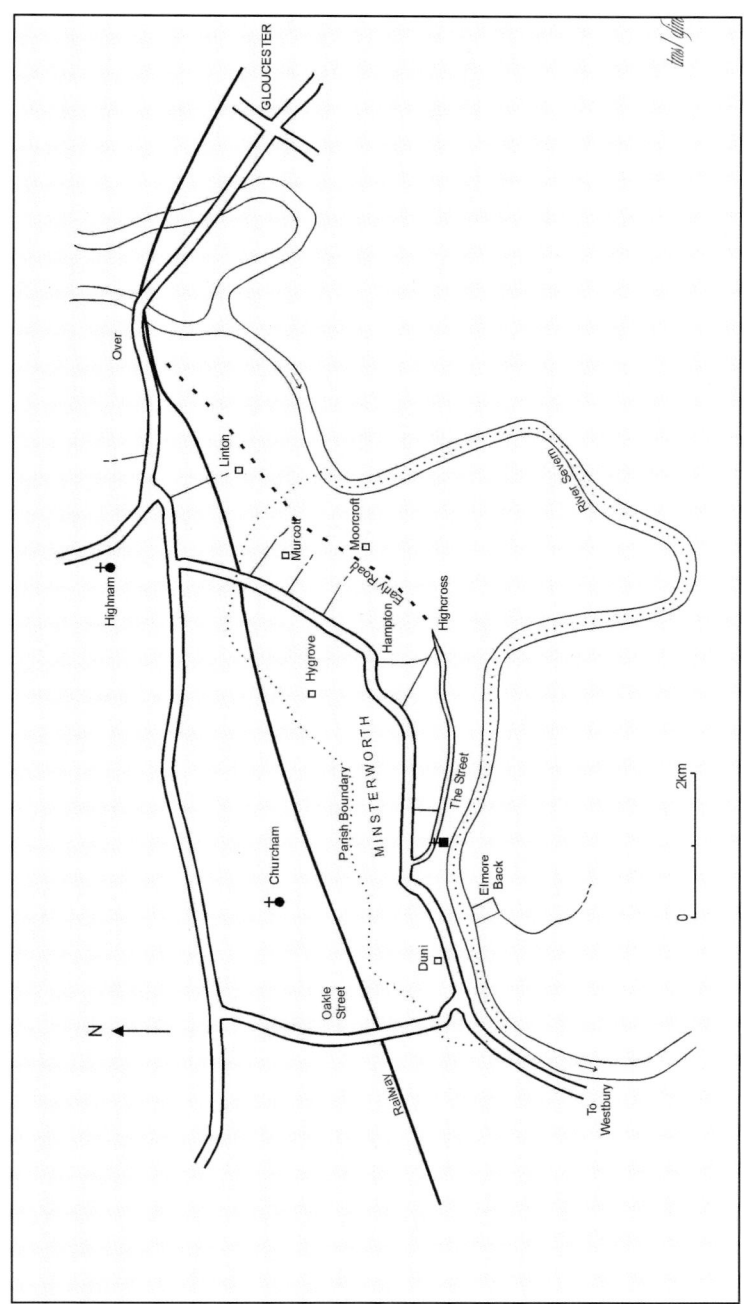

Sketch map of the historic parish of Minsterworth (Drawn by the author; computer graphics by D J Mayes)

I.
VICTORIAN MINSTERWORTH
(or ALL THINGS BRIGHT AND BEAUTIFUL)

Queen Victoria occupied the throne of England for well over 60 years from 1837 to 1901, making her the longest reigning monarch that this country has so far had. During her reign, Britain has been described as the wealthiest and most powerful nation on earth, greater even than the Roman empire. Building on the largely steam-driven industrial revolution of the 18th century, Britain continued to develop technologically: enormous advances took place in the steel and manufacturing industries as well as in agriculture, and transport was given a major boost with the introduction of the railways. A peak was reached in 1851 with the Great Exhibition in London, the grandness of which showed the whole world what a great technological and innovative power Britain had become.

Inevitably all this came at a social cost. Power had begun to shift from the aristocracy to a new wealthy middle class, leaders of industry and commerce. Gradually, many aspects of life came to be run by these newly privileged members of society who strongly espoused ideals of self-help and thrift. As for rural life, the arrival of cheap imports of foodstuffs (especially grain from North America) and the intensification of mechanisation on farms, created high levels of unemployment in the countryside. Many left their traditional home areas to seek work in the factories and mills of the new, often squalid, industrial towns. If unsuccessful there, the choice for many was either to starve or emigrate to the colonies. This is not to say that many ordinary people in villages like Minsterworth did not continue to thrive. The countryside was generally cleaner and more healthy and country folk could be a lot more self-sufficient.

The early 19th century traveller and journalist William Cobbett (d.1835) wrote in his book *RuralRides* that the country people he encountered:

> ...seemed to have been reasonably well-off: a pig in every cottage sty—that is the infallible mark of a happy people.

Much later in the century, in 1898, J Arthur Gibbs in his book *A Cotswold Village* wrote that:

> Most of the cottages are kept scrupulously clean; they have an air of homely comfort which calls forth admiration of all strangers. The children, too, when they go to school on Sundays, are dressed with a neatness and good taste that are simply astonishing when one recalls the income of a labourer...

Both these writers were of course relatively wealthy country gentlemen and it is perhaps typical that they should see country folk and their conditions in this rose-tinted way. The well-to-do gentry of Minsterworth over this period were mostly the property-owning families like the Evans's, later the Sym(e)s, of Hygrove, the Viner-Ellis's of Duni House and Severn Bank, and of course the Hawkins families. The wealth of all these families came partly from farming, from rented properties and land leased to tenant farmers, and from investments. In the case of the Viner-Ellis's, it also came from their large interests in fisheries.

William Cobbett encounters the local farm worker on his 'Rural Rides' (reproduced here under the terms of the Gutenburg E-book Licence).

Information on working class incomes in Minsterworth is scant, but around the country in 1850 an agricultural labourer could expect to receive about 8 to 9s a week and by 1890, for summer work, this had risen to 13s. Towards the end of the previous century the chronicler Arthur Young found that in this part of Gloucestershire a labourer could earn in winter 8 to 10d a week, at haymaking time 1s to 1s 8d and at harvest 1s plus board and cider. In the mid 1800s, William Viner-Ellis records paying a man for haymaking 10s a week with one gallon of cider per day. For mowing grass he paid 2s 6d an acre with 1 gallon of cider a day. It may also be a matter of interest to some that, for cleaning the 'common necessaries' (i.e. privies) he paid two men 7s 6d, while for cleaning the 'large and small necessaries' (probably the privies at Duni House) he paid £1. In 1830, the going rate for a three year contract with a mole-catcher was 4s.

Young also recorded how much he had to pay for basic foodstuffs in the places he visited. Around Minsterworth, bread was 2d per lb., butter 5d per lb., mutton and beef around 4d per lb. and bacon 8d per lb. Candles cost 7d a pound.

The local gentry and well-to-do farmers could not have been unaware of the hardships among village folk, particularly the agricultural labourers and their families and, as we shall see, they tried to be benevolent in a number of ways. The church also did what it could to help the poor. Under the Poor Law provisions, the Minsterworth parish vestry (until it was replaced by the modern parish council in 1894) had powers to help distressed people in the parish using Poor Rate contributions from parishioners. Beyond this, the poor and sick were forced to go into the local union workhouse and to suffer the degradation and hardships of life there.

For Minsterworth folk, the workhouse was in Westbury-on-Severn (the remnant of it can still be seen on the left hand side of the main street). Formed in 1835 and housing around 220 inmates, it also provided limited medical help from a resident physician. Fit inmates were put to mundane tasks such as the manufacture of pins (a major industry around Gloucester then) but they would still have had to live alongside the sick, dying, mentally ill, vagrants and orphaned children. It is recorded that during 1881 there were two people from Minsterworth in Westbury workhouse - a Thomas Brown aged 69, labourer, and Mary Oprirs, 9 years old and described as a scholar.

A verse from the hymn 'All things bright and beautiful', written in 1848, demonstrates peoples' attitude then:

> The rich man in his castle,
> The poor man at his gate,
> He made them, high or lowly,
> And ordered their estate.

The poor man at the gate was quite likely a candidate for the workhouse. This verse is now omitted from modern hymn books.

Minsterworth farm workers towards the end of the 19th century. Note the men's large reaping hooks and the wide bonnet that women wore as they worked in the fields.

During Victoria's reign though, conditions for ordinary folk did improve considerably. Major advancements occurred in the field of medicine giving people a much better chance of survival. Iodine, morphine and chloroform were developed and doctors began to link cholera to sewage and the importance of boiling drinking water and washing hands. Apart from their presence in the infirmaries and charitable hospitals, doctors were only available to those who could afford them. The same applied to sick persons requiring hospital treatment. We do know however, from numerous entries in his day-book covering the period 1824 to 1865, that William Viner-Ellis of Dun: House regularly recommended parishioners for treatment in Gloucester Infirmary. He was able to do this under regulations which allowed subscribers to the Infirmary, for each guinea paid per annum, the right to recommend one out-patient and one in-patient for treatment there each year. Over the forty odd years covered by the day-book, Mr Viner-Ellis records making in all 38 such recommendations.

For over a century before, there had also been local church charities aimed at improving the lot of the poor in Minsterworth and these continued in operation throughout most of the 19th century. The Hyett charity, first started in 1719, paid for local boys to be apprenticed to various trades, while the Wintle charity (founded in 1723) provided money for boots, linen, fuel and food to people in the parish not benefitting from Poor Law relief. For a time in the 1800s there was also the Evans charity which was used to distribute coal around the parish.

Impressive improvements in education also took place. Initially there was the Sunday school movement founded by Gloucester journalist and proprietor of the Gloucester Journal Robert Raikes (1736-1811). Before compulsory education arrived in 1870, these Sunday schools, which were run by both the Church of England and by non-conformist churches and funded by subscriptions, were a powerful means of spreading literacy among children all over the country. In Minsterworth parish, successive generations of children from both C of E and chapel backgrounds attended the Sunday school run by the Wesleyan chapel at Calcotts Green.

But moves to introduce better education for the village children had started much earlier than this with several legacies made by local persons in the latter half of the18th century. In 1763 Susannah Crump of Minsterworth had bequeathed £4 p.a. for a 'discreet' school mistress to teach 10 poor children in the parish to read. A school was founded in 1794 following a grant from the Hawkins family enabling up to 20 poor children from the parish to be educated. In 1784 land and further funds were donated for a school house to be built and maintained. That small red-brick building, which housed the schoolroom as well as accommodation for the school mistress, still stands in School Alley today; it displays a stone plaque showing the date 1808.

This is the earliest picture of Minsterworth school, taken around 1907, not so long after Queen Victoria died. Dress fashions had moved on but notice that one boy at least is still wearing the sailor suit that had been so fashionable during the Queen's reign.

Meanwhile, those who could afford it, paid to send their offspring to a school, usually one like the Crypt School in Gloucester. For example, in his daybook William Viner-Ellis regularly records paying out sums in the 1820s for his children's schooling. In 1824 he paid half-yearly fees of £96.14s.0d for three tutors at Crypt School. Over the next few years he paid sums of £37 and £54 per half year for four children and there was an extra £2 or so for dancing lessons.

Opportunities for leisure and recreation were limited compared to the wide range of activities available today. The working classes had little time for leisure and what did take place tended to be seasonal and mostly happened through the church and chapel, especially for religious celebrations, Harvest Home etc. Generally, concerts, fetes and parties (the latter often held in the schoolroom) would have been popular. It is recorded that the Wesleyan chapel regularly held tea parties on Calcotts Green each Spring. Visits to local markets and fairs would have had their attractions and, with the arrival of the railway, train excursions became possible. For some men, poaching provided a gainful, if often illegal, outlet.

From entries in Mr Viner-Ellis's daybook we know also that he regularly arranged religious meetings for bible readings and religious discussion; although serious in nature, these events would have been social occasions as well. Mr Ellis also writes about distributing religious books around the parish. In spite of the church's urgings on temperance, in time honoured Minsterworth tradition, many enjoyed regular convivial cider or perry drinking evenings in the various cider sheds which so many cottages and houses had. Alternatively, if they were so minded, men could have gone to one of the local licensed alehouses. Minsterworth itself had no public houses but there was a choice of the Bird In Hand (now the Severn Bore, recorded from as early as 1831), the Salmon Inn in Elmore Back and the Silent Whistle in Oakle Street (both licensed alehouses since at least 1891). An alehouse called the King's Head is also recorded as being at The Flat in Denny at least in the early 1800s.

Notes left to us by an earlier vicar of Minsterworth, record the generosity of Miss Ann Ellis, who in 1880 paid for repairs to the church bells and belfry, pointing out that:

> … the kind and considerate lady at whose expense the work was carried out had in view the improvement and innocent occupation of the young men and lads of the parish by giving some proportion of the leisure of their evenings to the practice of ringing ….

Very soon, the Minsterworth belfry team was quite successful, as the following illustration of a plaque in St Peter's church tower shows:

And, still today, ringers benefit from Miss Ellis's charity.

A picture taken at the turn of the century of the two Boyce girls, Annie and Amelia (both born in the mid-1880s) with their bicycles outside old Taterbury Cottage which used to be at The Naight near to Orchard End. Their father is believed to have been a farm labourer, suggesting that, by this later date, possession of bicycles by the less well-off was not unusual. (Photograph reproduced by courtesy of Mrs Cheryl Gobey).

Available records (including Mr Viner Ellis's diary) cast little or no light on leisure activities among the better-off and gentry of Minsterworth. They may well have indulged in some of the same entertainment as the lower classes (with the lower classes mostly keeping respectfully separate) but they had their own kind of pursuits. Visits to musical concerts and the theatre in Gloucester were possible and the Three Choirs Festival had already been around for over 100 years. The attractions of Cheltenham Spa were also tempting. Outdoor activities like hunting, fishing, archery, bicycling, croquet and tennis were popular, as were painting and embroidery for the ladies. Within their own class there was a fair amount of socialising among the leading local families who would also have been on close terms with the other notable families in the wider area such as the Colchester-Wemyss in Westbury, the Crawley-Boeveys at Flaxley and the Gambier Parrys of Highnam.

It is easy to imagine evening dinner parties or dances at one or other of the principle houses including listening to music and songs, playing whist and perhaps enjoying tableaux vivants (living pictures) where a group of guests, young and old, assumed suitable costumes and without speaking or moving, carefully posed to depict a particular theme.

A Victorian archery garden party (illustration from Cassell's Family Magazine of 1887).

One notable occasion for pleasure and festivities by everyone in Minsterworth and beyond was the celebration marking the consecration of the newly-built church of St Peter's in 1870. It was colourfully reported on in the Gloucester Journal of the day, which described how the church was elaborately decorated, flags fluttered from the church tower and the tallest trees. The account went on to say:

> As the hour fixed for the commencement of the service approached, the roads and lanes were filled with groups of parishioners and vehicles bringing the gentry and yeoman of the neighbouring villages .... The church was crowded in every part, admission being obtained by ticket....
> In the afternoon, luncheon was served in the schoolroom to upwards of 100 ladies and gentlemen. The vicar presided. The accommodation being inadequate to receive all comers at one sitting, the younger gentlemen were asked to air their hunger outside until the ladies had been attended to ...

How easy it is to imagine from this account how special this event was for the village and how it was enjoyed by all classes of person.

A chapel tea party in 1886, not in Minsterworth but in nearby Tibberton. No doubt though, the ladies and gentlemen of Minsterworth would have worn much the same style of costume. (Reproduced here by kind permission of Lawrence Davis of Tibberton.)

There is virtually no record of team sports being played in Victorian Minsterworth but some activities must have been engaged in by all classes of young men of the village. Cricket started to become popular in Britain from around 1850 and soon became a popular pursuit in most villages. Some form of football had always been played, but organised football clubs did not come along until later in the century and we know that the game locally had developed sufficiently for the Minsterworth Association Football Club to be set up in 1907.

If we were able to enter a time machine which could whisk us back to be an early Victorian traveller passing through Minsterworth, what impression of the village might we have had? Written records are available from two early travellers passing through the area a bit before this time. One was the Rev. F E Witts who was making his way on horseback to Ross-on-Wye in 1820, and the other was Arthur Young much earlier in 1767. Both admired the hilly, picturesque and fertile land beside the Severn river and Witts noted the distant view of May Hill. Neither mentions Minsterworth itself, but Young dwells at length on the dire state of the turnpike road from Gloucester to Newnham which would of course have taken him through Minsterworth. The early turnpike road engineers chose a zig-zag route for the new road following old field tracks on higher ground , by-passing much of old Minsterworth nearer the river, so that our early traveller may well not have realised the full extent of the settlement. For their part, the ordinary folk of the parish would probably have preferred to use the much older (and free) lower road through Murcott, Highcross and Calcotts Green down to Duni.

Using an 1839 map of Minsterworth, we can follow our traveller coming from the direction of the present-day Highnam roundabout. He would have spotted the small hamlets around Murcott to his left and the bold edifice of Highgrove to his right. The first buildings he would have encountered along the road were old Parlour Farm (where Redlands is today) and the building opposite it, now The Appletree Inn (remember that the modern housing along the main road up to this point did not come until the 1920/30s). Beyond there and until reaching Duni, all that he would have met along the road were the village pound and Pound Cottage, a blacksmith's forge near to where Rosedale now stands, Elm Farm and Lower Moorcroft Farm and Pump Court.

The Appletree Inn contains structures from many different dates but within the building are the remains of a cruck-framed open hall house dating from the late 15th/early 16th centuries, making it one of the oldest standing buildings in Minsterworth.

Almost 50 years later, according to the Ordnance Survey map of 1881, the only new sites to be seen were the school, the vicarage and Severn Bank.
Our visitor probably observed that, owing to the piecemeal way in which the

enclosure of the open common fields had happened over the preceding half century or so, there still remained areas of open fields with their traditional ridge and furrow strip cultivation: open fields like Oppithorne Field running down from the road towards Murcott and Upper Moorcroft and, further on, Climperland Field stretching to the north as far as the Longbrook.

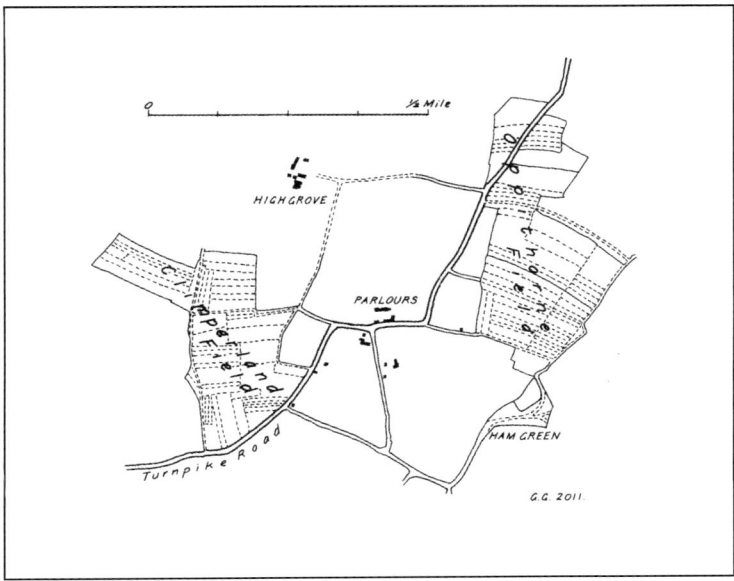

Map showing the alignment of the turnpike through Minsterworth (running from top right to bottom left) and also 'CLIMPERLAND FIELD' and 'OPPITHORNE FIELD' .
(Based on the 1839 Tithe Apportionment map for Minsterworth; reproduced by Geoffrey Gwatkin).

Without seeing the whole of the village, it would have come as a surprise to discover the size of population of the parish. Having been 354 in 1801, it had reached nearly 500 by 1851 (only to fall back to just over 400 by 1881). He might also have been intrigued by the fact that at this time the parish of Minsterworth also included land and property on the other side of the river at Elmore Back (described in one medieval record as 'Little Minsterworth across the water'), a situation that did not end until the creation of the new parish council in1894. Between Murcott in the east and Duni in the west, at least a dozen farms were in business. The 1851 national census (the first to give full details of every person) recorded three 'landed proprietors' (Messrs Ellis, Hawkins and Butt), 13 farmers and 65 agricultural labourers. Nor was Minsterworth short of its traders and craftsmen. In 1851, there were 7 carpenters in the village, 6 tailors, three stone masons and two blacksmiths.

Around 50% of the women listed were in domestic service and there were 14 registered 'paupers' receiving relief from the Parish Rate. Also in 1851, 8 fishermen and 2 mariners lived in Minsterworth. Later, in the 1870-80s, a baker and shoemaker operated in the village and a butcher (who also acted as a sub-postmaster) was recorded at Duni. We know from Mr Viner-Ellis' daybook that in 1862 telegraph poles were erected 'on the turnpike road opposite my dwelling (Duni House)', doubtless marking the arrival of a telegram service to the village postmaster's office.

The Corn Laws of 1846 had had an adverse effect on grain prices, but by the mid-1800s farming throughout the country was going through a relatively good period. Land owners and farmers were discovering the benefits of new methods of fertilization and of investing in improved drainage, whilst steam ploughing had begun to replace the centuries old horse- or bullock-drawn plough.

This well-built stone arched bridge crosses over a major drainage channel running from the Longbrook down to the river near Pershbrook. It carries an old farm road that led across the fields to Duni Farm which is still used by local farm traffic today. The quality of ashlar stonework and elegance of this bridge strongly suggests a 19th century date of construction, conceivably on the orders of William Viner-Ellis of Duni.

In Minsterworth and elsewhere locally, orchard growing and cider and perry production flourished. The produce was shipped out of the area both by river and by the new railway to South Wales. The contents of an auction sale of cider and perry at Duni Farm in 1898 amounted to 5,000 gallons of prime quality drink.

Fishing also remained important both for village folk anxious to find food for the family table, as well as for local entrepreneurs like William Viner-Ellis who received rent from his salmon fisheries on the river.

Our view of Victorian Minsterworth would be incomplete without brief consideration of how village people transported themselves and their goods. Most day-to-day movement around the village and to nearby towns and markets would have been on foot, perhaps with a handcart or donkey-cart to carry heavier loads. In the main though, people were heavily dependent on horse-drawn transport: wagons and carts for heavy loads, and various kinds of traps and carriages for carrying people. The turnpike road, when established early in the 18th century, was designed to provide a good surface for wheeled transport but even as Arthur Young records almost 50 years later:

> I was infinitely surprised to find the same stony, hard, rough and cursed roads, miscalled turnpikes, all the way from Gloucester to Newnham: it is the same stone as the other side of the Severne but much harder, and consequently more jolting and cutting to the horses feet; nor is it so much as level, but rutts all the way; and what is remarkable, I found by them, that they build their waggons with their wheels full three inches nearer to each other than in the eastern counties

An early 19th century carrier wagon, the equivalent of a modern-day bus service. It was used to carry goods and people. If asked, the carrier would also take items for special delivery. (Drawing of c.1820 taken from Thomas Burke's 'Travel In England' (1942))

During the 19th century the turnpike surface was gradually improved using stone obtained from local fields and Mr Viner-Ellis regularly notes fulfilling his 'statutory duty' to provide stone for road building (tarmac was known of in the 19th century but little used until the arrival of motor vehicles in the early 1900s). By the 1850s, two carriers passed through Minsterworth bound for Gloucester on 3 days a week, doubtless using the turnpike.

The maintenance of his carriage and horses regularly preoccupied Mr Viner-Ellis. On 13th April 1835, he notes "Began using the fly today" and mentions negotiations he was having with his driver, Benjamin Traveller, over ownership of his "cloathes" (i.e. uniform). Later we are told about the expenses involved in "shining and keeping supple the top part of the carriage" and of oiling it, as well as the costs of shoeing and feeding the horses. A little earlier in 1825, he had paid one guinea for a coach trip to London.

This is believed to be Mr John Clifford Stephens of Oakle House (1850-1945), a member of the Stephens' family of The Naight in Minsterworth. Note the liveried groom holding the horse.

The 50th year of Queen Victoria's reign, 1887, was marked with a Golden Jubilee of public celebration throughout the whole country. Naturally, Minsterworth was not going to be left out of the celebrations. According to a local newspaper, the Jubilee was celebrated in Minsterworth in a large meadow belonging to Mr William Littleton (of Duni Farm). At the entrance gate, there was an arch of evergreen, flowers and flags with pictures of the Queen and "Long May She Reign!". About 260 parishioners sat down to dinner in a large tent, Mr Viner-Ellis presiding, and enjoyed "the good old side of beef and plum pudding, ale and cider, which has done so much to build up the British character." Speeches followed extolling the Queen's many virtues, advancements made during her reign in the conditions of the lower and middle classes, the arrival of the railways, cheap postage and the electric telegraph. The healths of the vicar Mr Balfour and of the Squire Mr Ellis were drunk with great gusto and amidst cheers. This was followed by dancing, races run for Jubilee medals and a tug-of-war.

The Queen was to live for another 14 years but the 20th century was just around the corner. With it came the demise of the old country squire-archy, leaving rural communities feeling anxious for the future, and a new era of remarkable technological progress. Nor could anyone then have anticipated the imminent Great War which came as a bombshell upon the lives of local communities. But, on that day in 1887 at least, the folk of Minsterworth were just enjoying being Victorians!

II.
THE "HOUSE" THAT DANIEL BUILT

In around 1757, the recently arrived lord of the manor of Minsterworth Sir Charles Barrow Bart. built himself a "capital mansion" in the then-popular classical style on high ground in the north of the parish in an area previously known as Hampton. He called the house Hygrove and it was to be his family seat and centre of his Minsterworth manorial estate. At that time, he probably had little idea that one of his tenants who had taken a lease on a farm in Duni, at the other end of the parish, would one day build himself a grand house every bit as splendid as Hygrove. Nor could Sir Charles have predicted that this tenant would go on to establish a local family dynasty that for the best part of two centuries would make a profound mark on the economic and social life of Minsterworth, rivalling that of any lord of the manor.

The story starts 250 years ago with a Daniel Ellis senior of Elmore, a member of an Ellis family associated with Elmore since at least the 16th century. They appear to have made their money principally through the sale of fish. In 1738, he married a Susannah Crump, probably the daughter of William Crump who, in the 1720s, held property in Minsterworth, including a pastureland in Duni known as Averidge and the fishery there. Daniel died in 1764 and his inheritance passed to a son also called Daniel. By the 1750s, Duni Farm, recorded as being part of Minsterworth manor, was leased out to Daniel Ellis Gent. and in 1757 the site at Duni is described as "Ellis's homestead". (See map overleaf).

That he was referred to as "Gent" reflects that by this time a degree of respectability already attached to him. Around this time he married a Mary Viner, possibly from the Viner family associated with Gloucester and Badgeworth. This union may well have brought in additional means to enable the Ellis's to improve on their possessions. It also resulted in descendants of the family adopting the combined name of Viner Ellis (interestingly, a memorial to a daughter Mary, located in the tower room of Minsterworth church, describes her parents as Daniel Ellis and Mary Viner). Daniel also had his philanthropic side since, in a will proved in 1784, he left £100 towards setting up a new school for the village (about twenty years earlier, Susannah Crump - either his mother or grandmother - had also made an endowment towards the school) (see Chapter I).

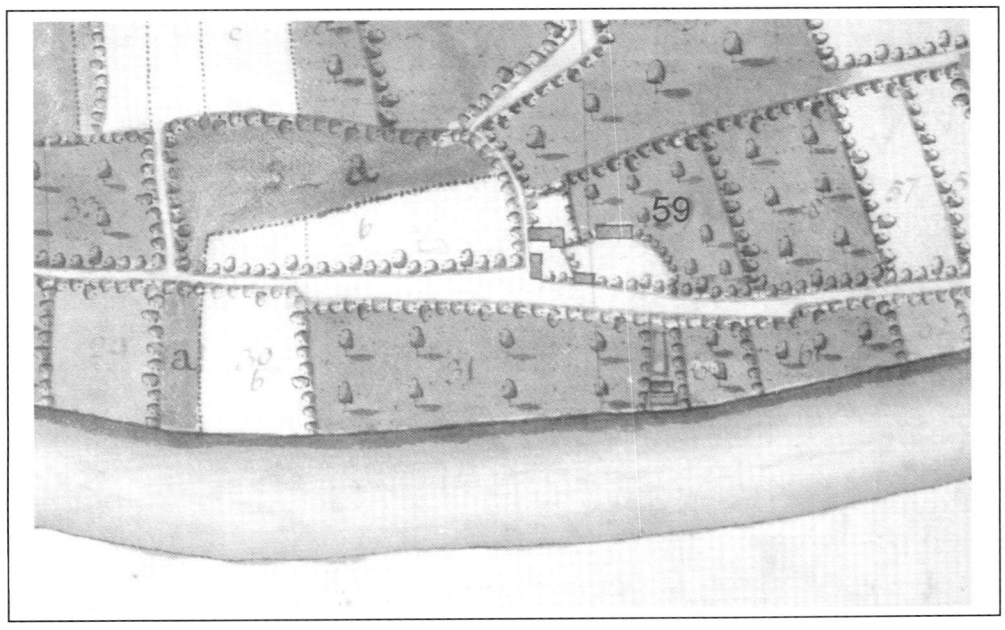

Detail from a 1757 estate map of Minsterworth. Field no.59 and the buildings on it equate to "Ellis's homestead".

Daniel Ellis died in 1797 (four years after Mary) but before that, in 1783, in a part of that same field called Averidge, just west of Duni Farm, he built a fine new house which for much of its life would be owned and occupied by successive generations of the Viner Ellis family. This was an impressive three-storey brick and stone house built in the elegant fashion of the time with two prominent front bays extending over all three floors.

Initially, the house was probably known simply as "Ellis's place" but on Bryant's 1824 map of Gloucestershire, it is distinctly entitled "Minsterworth Ho." (it would become known as Duni House much later). There is a fascinating hand-written account relating to the building of the house submitted to Mr & Mrs Ellis by a surveyor (Richard Goodman of Lydney) dated January 22 1783. It lists in great detail aspects of work done: the brick and stone work, tiling and carpenters' work, the quantity of materials used and the times taken on each piece of work (for example foundations, walls, at least four chimneys, window frames, doors and so on). There are repeated references to a lower floor, a middle floor and an upper floor.

Daniel Ellis's house at Duni, as it appeared in later times. The house no longer exists, but the cedar tree protruding into the picture (top left corner) still stands beside the road.

All does not appear to have gone smoothly however. In what is clearly a dispute over payment, Mr Goodman writes in a somewhat aggrieved tone:

Mrs Ellis.
> The inclosed is the whole charge I have Against you and a Very Reasonable one, and I am sure I have don you Justice in Every Respect and you have a compleat house built wholly under my Directions for which I have charged you the small sum of fifteen Guinneas for all my Troubbles of surveying and managing the same, including Putting up your Cyder [barn?] and Papering your parlour and if I had charg'd You the full worth of my Trouble and drawing I could not have char g'd you less than 30 Guinneas As I think [you and] Mr Ellis have no reason to think but it is Reasonable Enough but I never did a Jobb before But I had all my Board Entirly nor never will.
>
> And I am suppris'd that Mr Ellis could Expect as I can Give him all my Trouble and Time in Managing his Building as no Gentleman Nor Tradesman in the Kingdom besides would have [-] it for you know all the whole lay on me Entirley and as to my Part I will not take one Farthing of the charge for if it be

(continued overleaf)

> judg'd by surveyors I shall be allowed a deal more for Everthing As I am willing to have don by any able surveyor And I desire as the matter stands and Mr Ellis have [-] of my man that you will settle the whoie matter with him as I Give him   full Power in My behalf and that he may settle with Every body And have Recaits (i.e. receipts) from Everyone that I have any Concern with the Jobb on my account
> From your Most obliged Humble [servant] To command
> R Goodman
> Lidney Jan'ry the 22 1783

Unfortunately, we do not know the outcome of all this—one assumes that Mr. Goodman was duly paid for all his pains!

Daniel had four sons but the eldest, also Daniel, took up medicine away from Minsterworth and after his death in 1797, the estate passed to his second son William, then aged 21. William had continued his father's fishery business and, by 1800, the family were described as "fishmongers" at Duni House. He appears also to have embarked on enlarging his estate (probably taking advantage of the gradual breaking up of the Hygrove estate) so that by the middle of the 19th century he was firmly established as one of the principal landed proprietors of Minsterworth and a member of the local "gentry". A measure of the family's standing and degree of self-respect around this time is that in 1812 William applied for and was granted a coat of arms. Its motto, Je Vive en Espoir, translates as I Live in Hope.

William seems to have embodied all the virtues of a typical benevolent country 'squire' but what was William the person really like? Sadly no portraits from the time have emerged to help us but, as touched on in the previous chapter, among the Viner Ellis family's archive is a hand-written daybook or diary of William Viner Ellis senior providing a remarkably informative insight into the day-to-day preoccupations and concerns of this Victorian country gentleman spanning the years 1824 to 1864. We read of his enthusiasm for planting trees (typically sycamore, cedars and auricaria (monkey puzzle)) in the grounds at Duni House, on the land opposite called Plackett Pool, and at Severn Bank. He also notes the building at Duni in 1829 of the garden wall, of the costs of school fees for his growing family (eventually six in all, including one boy at Crypt School Gloucester), costs of having fields mowed and income from the sale of hay, cider and perry, and his concern over the proper care and maintenance of his carriages and horses. Also reflected are his interests in local fisheries (including those at Framilode, Rodley and the leasing out of fishing rights. Such was his interest in this that in 1831 he recorded visiting

Parliament in London "to attend a Bill for the better regulating of salmon fisheries in England and Wales".

The Viner Ellis coat of arms (reproduced by courtesy of Mrs Felicity Karger)

His public-spirited side is also evident: he often writes of recommending a local parishioner to be treated at Gloucester Infirmary and of his participation in local church affairs, including distributing religious books from his own personal library. Bible reading meetings were regularly held at both Duni House and Severn Bank.

Among the entries in his book are these, which seem to take us just a bit closer to the man:

>Clock: if it should lose, screw pendulum up; if gain, let it down.

>Gift to Mr William Barrett of 12 [bottles] of port wine for serving as officer of the Guardians of the Poor (1845).

(continued overleaf)

> [At] 5.55a.m. started walk with daughter Anne into 6 parishes—completed by 7.30p.m., in my 80th year, done without feeling any fatigue. WVE (May 1856)
>
> First truss in my 84th year (June 1860).

The final entry in the diary was in October 1865 and he died later that same year.

As well as two daughters, William senior and his wife Elizabeth produced five sons. Of these, William junior (1809-1888), who took over the family estate and role of "squire", was a solicitor and also for a time alderman and then mayor of Gloucester. His elder brother George (1812-1900) entered the medical profession, aspiring to be Doctor, later Professor, of Anatomy at University College London. Between 1852 and 1873, The London Times contained various reports on his anatomical publications as well as his election first as examiner in Anatomy at University College and eventually as Dean of the faculty. There was also Edmund (1819-1903), who took up banking in Gloucester.

William junior carried on in the same mould as his father and under him the family's estate continued to prosper. By the late 1800s, the Viner Ellis properties included Duni House, Minsterworth Court, Murcott Farm, Tithe Cottage and numerous lesser properties and land in the parish. Also around 1860, at Severn Bank, a new large dwelling house was built replacing an earlier dwelling near the site; this house was eventually acquired by brother George as his retirement home which he shared with his two sisters. William's will dated 1887 contains a reference to what was still the main seat of the Viner Ellis's in Minsterworth:

> … my dwelling house called Duni House, with Plackett Pool Orchard and land called Averidge.

Documents show that, at the time of his death in 1888, he also possessed Highleadon Court, farms in Taynton, Churcham and Herefordshire and property in Westbury.

We have already seen that William was also successfully engaged in local politics but not everything seems to have gone quite well for him in that sphere. Several issues of The London Times between 1857 and 1859 contain reports of hearings of the Gloucester Election Commission where allegations of electoral bribery were made against him in his capacity of agent for the local Liberal MP candidate (and brother-in-law). This on 25th July 1857 for example:

> …. A fishmonger George Bullock was asked for his vote by Mr Viner Ellis. Bullock said he had had bad luck lately with his fish and Mr Ellis who was owner of large fisheries said if he voted for Mr Price he should not want for fish. Mr Viner Ellis denied this.

In October 1859 Mr Viner Ellis was again mentioned in reports alleging payment of money for votes. But he does not appear to have suffered much damage from these episodes which were probably far from uncommon in the political life of the time.

As this extract from a tribute to him in a local newspaper of 1888 shows though, he was also known for his good works:

> He was also a Non-conformist, and was more or less intimately connected with the Congregational church in Gloucester for at least half a century…....When the present handsome chapel was erected, some 35 years ago, he was reported to have been the largest contributor to the funds.

The same article goes on to point out that his gifts to the church were not restricted to the Non-conformists. He was a major contributor to several imposing stained glass windows in Gloucester's cathedral and also presented the illuminated clock for the tower of St Peter's Catholic church at Gloucester.

As to Minsterworth, the same article states:

> The new parish church was built in 1869-70, and, as the chief landowner, he contributed £600 to the funds, while his sisters the Misses Ellis, and his brothers, Mr G Viner Ellis and Mr E Viner Ellis gave between them an additional £700, together nearly one-half the cost of the new edifice. Mr Ellis also provided two or three mission-rooms in the widely-extending parish of Westbury-on-Severn and at Bulley. In early life Mr Ellis was a man of remarkably active habits, and it is said he walked from Gloucester to London, over 100 miles, in two days, sleeping at Oxford on the journey…....As the owner of valuable fisheries, he took much interest in the preservation of salmon in the Severn; while, as a landowner in a famous fruit-growing district, he was unwearied in introducing improved varieties of apples, pears and plums into this county.

His popularity among the villagers themselves is in little doubt. There is another local newspaper report from 1887, this time concerning a grand celebration and dinner in Mr Littleton's meadow at Duni Farm which was presided over by Mr Ellis. We are told that:

> After the vicar's toast to the Queen's good health, the health of the Squire
> Mr Ellis was drunk with gusto and amidst cheers.

At this point in the story, one might be excused wondering whether things could continue being so good for the Viner Ellis's.

The fact though is that, like so many of the landed gentry of England at this time, the Viner Ellis's income was heavily dependent on agriculture and rents from tenants. Throughout the late Victorian period farming had been in slow decline not least because of the growth of foreign imports of grain. Earlier investments in land had left landowners in debt, and burdensome taxation added to the decline in their fortunes. The old order was changing and giving away to the modern era of industry, commerce and social change. It had become a hard time for farmers and landowners to be successful.

George Viner Ellis of Severn Bank died in 1900 and, out of the rest of the Viner Ellis's, it was his nephew Godfrey William (son of Edmund Viner Ellis) who emerged as the most prominent member of the family locally. Only a year earlier he had married Margaret Hannah, the daughter of James Raine, a residentiary canon and chancellor of York cathedral. Now known by the surname Viner Vyner Ellis, they continued to occupy Duni House but also used a house in Lymington in Hampshire. Sadly, in 1911 Godfrey died when only 47 years old leaving behind Margaret with their two children William and Margery. At this point, Margaret took up residence in The Court where she remained until her death in 1958. The reason for Godfrey changing his surname to Vyner Vyner Ellis is not clear; nor is it obvious why Margaret after 1911 decided to be known by the surname Vyner Ellis.

Before concluding the tale of Daniel Ellis's "house" however, we should focus briefly on Margaret of Minsterworth Court for she can reasonably be said to have successfully carried the family's standing a good way into the 20th century. She is certainly not a forgotten local figure from the past. Her grand-daughter,

Felicity (now Felicity Karger living in Oakle Street) fondly remembers her 'granny'- as no doubt do her other grand daughters Primrose and Morwenna, who still have interests in Minsterworth. There may even be some folk in the village who remember how she hosted the annual church fetes and presided at the regular annual Minsterworth Horticultural Show and her support to the local school.

Godfrey William Viner Ellis (d. 1911) and Mrs Margaret Vyner Ellis (d.1958).

She was well known for her passion for daffodils, which she grew extensively in the Court gardens, and her work in this field was recognised nationally when she was registered by the Royal Horticultural Society as a significant person in the daffodil world. For some years she was a churchwarden and prominent benefactor at St Peters church and it was she who originated the idea of, and worked tirelessly to bring about, the building of the Memorial (now the Village) Hall which was opened in 1928. Her time as " leading lady" of Minsterworth encompassed two World Wars which inevitably impacted on local village life. In particular, as the following extracts from parish magazines during WWI show, Margaret took a prominent role in supporting the local war effort :

> Mrs Vyner Ellis, with her usual kind thoughtfulness, has presented to each one who has enlisted from this parish a very handsome knife with chain attached. Now! Let the Germans beware. (October 1914)

> The Red Cross Working Party has done, and is doing, good work. Last week Mrs Vyner Ellis took into the Infirmary, as a result of the workers' efforts, 34 very well made and warm flannel shirts. Many other warm mufflers, socks etc. are being made by members of the Working Party. (December 1914)

By December 1916 (with the national mood still patriotic but now much less buoyant) we learn from the magazine that a church Volunteer Training Corps had been formed and that Mrs Viner Ellis was sometimes called upon to review them on parade. She is also reported as making a gift of a service rifle to one member of the Corps for his successes on the rifle range.

Members of the Minsterworth Volunteer Training Corps probably photographed in the gardens of Minsterworth Court sometime during WWI.

Under Godfrey's will made in 1911, all of his property was bequeathed to family trustees (including Margaret Hannah) upon trust for sale and conversion as agreed. Various members of the family maintained residences at properties in the village such as The Court, Tithe Cottage and Cray Croft but, following the demise of George and his two sisters, Severn Bank soon passed into different hands. In 1914, a Mrs Fielden is recorded as an occupant (probably a tenant) at Duni House. Initially, in 1925, the house (along with other Viner Ellis properties) was put up for sale, apparently unsuccessfully. For three successive years between 1924 and 1926 there were to-let notices in The LondonTimes , the following (from 28 August 1926) being typical:

> **To Let.** Unfurnished charming fair-sized COUNTRY HOUSE,
> f our miles Gloucester; three large sitting rooms, seven bedrooms, bath;
> telephone; good kitchens and servant's sitting room; vinery, garage,

(continued overleaf)

stabling, carriage drive and lodge; double tennis court; first rate gardens (man and boy sufficient); beautiful views and orcharding; in all seven acres. Rent £150 p.a. on lease or £130 without orchard. All particulars from Mrs Vyner Ellis, Minsterworth Court. No agents.

Another advertisement in 1927 made mention also of:

…. A walled in kitchen garden with prolific figs, peaches and apricots.

A local directory for 1939 notes the occupant at Duni House as Mr Noel Viner-Brady.

As to the fate of Duni House during its final years, local resident and historian Margaret Winstone recalls (the added dates are my own):

It was a house in the grand style with a beautiful walled garden (parts of which can still be seen) but the house was demolished [in 1965]. I remember it well when [in about 1939] the Viner Brady family lived in one part and the Misses Outram in the other….. The house was then vacant for a long while until [in 1947] Miss Mary Vining from Churcham bought it and opened it up as a licensed guest house named The Grange. She was later joined by her brother Jack and his family but its revival was rather short-lived. Many items of great value were put on view and for sale by the late Arthur Negus. It then fell into disrepair and [in 1965] eventually demolished to become part of Duni Farm as it is today.

For at least some of this final period, the house was known as The Grange Hotel and there is a copy of a bill dated 15th May 1949 which, under the heading of "Grange Hotel", refers to the proprietors as John Chamberlayne and Mary Vining. The bill was for one night's bed and breakfast for two (with breakfast served in the room) together with other meals and drinks, the whole coming to £4.15s.4d.!

Sadly, although the old garden wall from 1829 is still in place, the actual house that Daniel Ellis built, and must have had such pride in, has gone. Nevertheless, as long as there are Viner Ellis's around (and ideally living in Minsterworth), his lineage remains with us—and long may it be so. The legacy of Daniel and his descendants are around us still: in the houses and other buildings which they built or contributed towards building, the old large ornamental trees still around Plackett Pool and Severn Bank, names on gravestones in the churchyard, and even in the husbanded landscape around us which they had such a big hand in shaping.

III.

JUST A PIECE OF OLD CLOTH

In its newly-conserved condition, it hangs inside a glass–fronted display case in the south west corner of the nave in St Peter's parish church Minsterworth. To the casual viewer, it may look just like an old piece of embroidered cloth, but there is much more to it than meets the eye. So, gentle reader, read on.

'Opus Anglicanum' and the Minsterworth Embroidery

The style of early English needlework and embroidery known as 'Opus Anglicanum' (English Work) dates back to Anglo Saxon times and flourished particularly between the 12th and 14th centuries. By that time it was famous all over Europe for its excellence and it was employed in the making of ecclesiastical and secular clothing, hangings and other textile articles. Gold and silver threads and coloured silks were applied on to silk or linen material to achieve marvellous combinations of design and colour. Some of this work was carried out by men (mostly monks) but mainly it was done either by nuns in convents or ladies of high status desirous of some occupation and amusement. Later in the period, the highest quality work was produced in professional workshops in London employing both men and women.

Perhaps the most celebrated piece of such work is the 11th century Bayeux Tapestry which dramatically depicts events leading up to the Norman invasion of England as well as the invasion itself. Its origins have been the subject of much speculation. In France, it was traditionally held to have been commissioned and created by Queen Matilda, wife of William The Conqueror. More recent research however has found evidence that it was more likely commissioned by William's half brother, Bishop Odo, whose main power base was actually in Kent and that the work was undertaken by Anglo Saxon artists and seamsters.

In the 13th century numerous pieces of the work were in the Vatican. In 1246,

Detail from the Bayeux Tapestry showing William at a banquet, surrounded by his barons and Bishop Odo.

Pope Innocent IV, observing certain beautiful vestments, enquired where they were made and, hearing that they were made in England (Opus Anglicanum), exclaimed:

Truly, England is our garden of delight

…. and letters were sent out calling on all abbots to procure many more such embroidered vestments for the Vatican.

Only a small proportion of this English Work has survived. Many articles fell victim to fire, war and the ravages of time. Worn-out articles could be burned to extract the precious metals used in their manufacture. But the greatest toll was exacted at the Reformation when the making of ecclesiastical embroideries in England all but ceased.

The Minsterworth embroidery itself can be best described as a patchwork of materials from different time periods made up into a panel measuring approximately 46 by 61 inches. Some of the pieces at least appear to derive from a chasuble or dalmatic which were garments worn by priests, the original shoulder area of the garment now being about a quarter of the way down the panel.* The panel consists of pieces of fine red velvet decorated with various appliqué embroidered motifs of a

---

* The **chasuble** is a liturgical vestment worn by clergy for celebration of the Eucharist or Mass in traditional Christian churches. It originated as a sort of conical poncho, i.e. an oval piece of cloth with a round neck hole in the middle, extending to below the knees. It was later shortened to reach no lower than the wrists. The **dalmatic** is a similar garment but with sleeves and open sides.

type fashionable in England in the first half of the 16th century prior to the Reformation. These include seraphim standing on wheels, fleur de lys, stylised flowers and double-headed eagles. Running from top to bottom is a narrow band or 'orphrey' strip bearing images of four figures: a saint with cross and book, a king with sceptre, Saint Paul with sword and book and an Old Testament figure, each one standing inside a Gothic architectural niche. These orphreys are also identified as being work from the first half of the 16th century. The two side edges and bottom edge of the panel are bordered with a patterned tawny coloured fabric probably of the early 17th century and possibly of N. France origin.

The Minsterworth embroidery on display in St Peter's church, Minsterworth

The original neck hole of the garment has been filled in with a patch of embroidery depicting part of a crucifixion scene (the torso of Christ on the Cross and a watching angel). It so happens that this patch can be linked to a large embroidered former altar cloth in St Peter's church Winchcombe. That embroidery is composed mainly of orphrey figures, very like those at Minsterworth, and also a crucifixion scene. The image of the crucifixion however has a missing portion which has been substituted with some other material. Quite remarkably, it is clear that the missing piece from the Winchcombe crucifixion was used to fill in the neck hole of the Minsterworth chasuble!

Detail of the patched neck-hole of the Minsterworth chasuble. The angel is on the left with Christ's torso section to the right.

Because the border of the Winchcombe embroidery contains the design of a pomegranate, a connection has been drawn between it and Queen Katherine of Aragon, the first wife of Henry VIII, whose emblem was the pomegranate. It may be a step too far to associate these embroideries as the work of Queen Katherine or her entourage of ladies, but the link with Winchcombe may at least suggest a connection either with the abbey there or nearby Hailes abbey. It would also appear that at some time in the past the two embroideries were in the same hands.

There is however an alternative theory which links up the Minsterworth embroidery to a number of other such examples existing in this part of the country and a journey made in 1502 by Queen Elizabeth, wife of Henry VII (1485-1509), into West Gloucestershire and Gwent. It is recorded that she stopped at Flaxley abbey, Monmouth and Raglan castle. The return journey into England however was somewhat ill-fated: much of her baggage was lost or couldn't be conveyed back across the Severn and had to return to Berkeley via Gloucester. Some of her precious possessions and their guardians were left behind at Minsterworth. Still preserved are ancient embroidered chasubles in churches at Monmouth and Abergavenny (the latter said to have been concealed at Raglan castle), a fine cope at Skenfrith and other articles at Littledean and Usk. The queen was known as a devout and generous lady making offerings and giving gifts wherever she stayed. Could this explain the presence of so many such vestments in these parts?

The Monmouth Chasuble, back view. Along with other vestments, it was cut up and kept in obscurity until finally, in the 19th century, being reassembled.

We may never find out for sure the origins of the Minsterworth embroidery, but one thing is certain: its eventual destiny, like that of so many other ecclesiastical vestments and other church treasures throughout the country, was drastically affected by the Reformation and its injunctions.

The Reformation and its Impact on Minsterworth Church

Recall the last time you visited a small rural Roman Catholic church in France or one of the other European countries having a catholic tradition and try to remember the appearance of its interior and its general atmosphere. This quite probably is how the parish church in Minsterworth would have looked before the Reformation. The dedication of the church in medieval times was to St George but we know that lit candles could be found in the church not just to St George but also to Mary The Virgin, St Katharine, St Clement, St Thomas and St Nicholas as well as to The Holy Cross. Each of these dedications probably had its own niche altar or shrine in the church complete with images of the saint and with lamps always lit around each of the altars and around the rood screen. Even a small church like ours would have possessed an amount of gold or silver plate and other precious goods, including highly embellished vestments, chasubles and possibly copes. The interior walls would have been decorated with paintings on sacred themes and hung with banners.

For its upkeep the church relied heavily upon money that came from its chantries. Each particular chantry in the church was founded to pay for priests to say prayers and sing masses for the souls of departed parishioners and they provided the means whereby individual parishioners or groups of parishioners (often known as 'guilds') could make financial endowments to the church. We believe that a chantry chapel of the medieval de Minsterworth family stood on the north side of the chancel. In the case of Minsterworth church also, one source that casts light on this arrangement is to be found in the opening lines of wills made by local villagers. In 1508, one Richard Colyns of Minsterworth instructed in his will that he be:

> buried in the chauncell before thymage of St George. [He endowed] to the high alter 20d. To the St George light 8d. To Our Lady and the lights of the Roode, St Kateryn, St Clement, St Thomas and St Nicholas 8d each…. My wife shall fynde a secular priest to syng in the said parish churche att thaulter of Our Lady for oon hole yere for the souls of John Colyns and Agnes, my fader and moder, and for William Colyns, my broder…..

Money would also have come from rentals on land possessed by the church and granted to it *in perpetuity* for its upkeep. A local field name that repeatedly appears in old documents from the 16th century onwards is the Lampe Half Acre field, a small meadow (possibly in Cornham) the rent from which had once been bequeathed to the chantry of St Mary in Minsterworth 'for the maintenance and findinge' of three lamps to burn in the church.

As in all parishes around the country, the church's festivals were eagerly participated in by the parishioners especially the church's saint days (of which there were many in the year). On these saint days or 'holydays', no work was done in the parish and the 'wakes' held to celebrate the event involved much eating, drinking and revelling. The people's indulgence, often to excess, on these occasions can be appreciated better when we think that these festivals provided the only break they had from the day-to-day hardship of life.

"The Kermesse of St George": by the Flemish artist Peter Bruegel The Younger (ca.1564-1636), produced in 1628. The term 'kermesse' or 'kermis' referred to the saint's day celebration (in this case for St George) held in most Catholic communities throughout the middle ages. Whether St George's Day was celebrated in this way in Minsterworth is not known.

Sadly for them, as part of his drive to change the national religion, King Henry VIII in 1532 abolished these holydays and local festivals throughout the land because of the 'decay of industry and the encouragement of sloth, idleness and sins of the flesh' they brought about.

This though was just one small step towards much more radical changes to the English church. In so many ways, the church had been at the centre of life for all and the fundamental changes brought about by the Reformation were to alter the way of life that people had known and taken for granted for the best part of 1000 years.

King Henry VIII's desire to divorce from his queen Katherine of Aragon and to obtain a male heir at whatever cost (known at the time as 'The King's Great Matter') was certainly a major factor in the drive to break from Rome and secure for Henry supremacy over the church in England. There were other reasons though. The king was short of money to pay both for his extravagant life at court and to meet the heavy cost of a war with France. He had come to resent the wealth, power and splendour of the monasteries with their estates, magnificent buildings and enormous influence. Additionally, this situation coincided with a Europe-wide surge of Protestantism which was gaining followers in England.

In the early 1530s, led by Henry's chief minister Thomas Cromwell, attacks were in full swing against the Catholic worship of the saints, of their relics and images and the practice of indulgences. Injunctions were issued exhorting people to put their trust instead into charity, mercy and faith. The principal targets at this stage however were the monasteries. In 1535, royal commissioners began visitations to assess all the smaller houses (those with an income of less than £200p.a.) and, a year later, a law was passed dissolving them all. Pressure was then put on the larger houses and gradually, one by one, these all succumbed and their wealth dropped into the hands of the State and its officials. By 1540 all monastic institutions, abbeys and convents had been dissolved, their relics destroyed and all their possessions removed: the lead from their roofs, bells, jewels, precious plate and beautiful vestments. Their buildings were razed to the ground or sold off for secular use and few survived intact. The priory of St Oswald's in Gloucester, which sponsored Minsterworth church, met a similar fate. A few abbey buildings survived like Gloucester's St Peter's and Bristol's St Augustine's through their being converted into cathedrals.

The small local parish churches meanwhile, having lost the patronage of local monasteries on which they relied, were reduced to a state of poverty and uncertainty about the future. The final blow to the parish churches came in 1547 (with the young Protestant King Edward VI now on the throne) when a law was passed abolishing all chantries, and the endowments and guilds that went with them and ordering visits to every parish to ensure all the shrines and images were destroyed. The publication of a new Book of Common Prayer was another attempt to break with the past, one element of it being that the communion service should no longer be celebrated by a priest wearing traditional vestments (the chasuble in particular being associated with the mass). Minsterworth people may have been slow to accept these injunctions since local wills at the time continue to specify endowments to various altar services in the church and to the provision of lights.

By around 1549 however some elements of the new way of thinking had begun to enter into Minsterworth wills: that of John Cowley in 1548 for example reads:

> ….. My soule to God. To be buryed in the churche yarde of Saynt George of Minsterworth. To the Cathedral churche of Gloucester 4d. To the reparacyon of the churche of Minsterworth 4d.

Other wills around this time reflect endowments being made towards the repair of the West Bridge in Gloucester, to the 'pore man's boxe' and to prisoners in Gloucester jail. By now the mass and all its trappings, vestments etc. had been abolished, altars torn down, walls whitened and stained glass windows broken up. There are records of churchwardens around the country disposing of their church's valuables initially to raise funds but later also dispersing them around the parish for safe keeping to avoid the expected confiscation. Quite often, church vestments and plate were forcibly removed by the local gentry.

By 1549 the situation with regard to Minterworth's finances had been reached where the churchwardens were obliged to submit a plea to the church authorities that they be allowed to use:

> …… rents which at some times had been employed toward finding of a priste bestowed by (with no small portion of their own goods) to repare of sea walls—if not done, rages of the water will break in and drown a great part of the said parish to the inhabitants' utter undoing. [We beg] the king's special grace in this behalf towards the continuall charges ….. as your worshippes are more at large certified [to approve] by the commissioners appointed for chantries, guilds &c. in [this] county.

The premature death of the young King Edward in 1553 brought to the throne the staunchly Catholic queen, Mary, daughter of Henry and Katherine of Aragon, and those churchmen who had previously been minded to think that the new-fangled Protestantism wouldn't last had grounds to feel vindicated. Virtually overnight, the nation had to revert to the fundamentals of Catholicism: the traditional latin primer

A present-day Catholic shrine to Our Lady as might have existed in the north aisle of Minsterworth church before the Reformation.

was re-introduced and injunctions were issued throughout the land to have all the old books, vessels and vestments provided in churches. As a consequence, many of the sacred objects removed during Edward's reign were brought out of their various places of concealment and restored to the churches. There was of course a dark side to the 'Marian Reaction' which smacked very much of the Spanish Inquisition. Whereas the punishment for treason was beheading, for heresy it was burning at the stake. During Mary's short 5-year reign, almost 300 Protestant 'heretics' were martyred in this way, including bishop John Hooper who suffered horribly at the stake in Gloucester in 1555. Such persecutions though only served to exacerbate anti-Catholic feeling among the people.

1558 saw the death of Mary and the accession of the Protestant Elizabeth I to the throne. This change was to bring about what was a third major church transformation in barely a dozen years. The 1559 Act of Uniformity abolished the mass (again) and re-introduced the Edward prayer book. Checks were made on all parish churches to ensure that the recently re-acquired objects of Catholicism were once again taken away and destroyed. At first there was some relaxation over the use of vestments but in time these too had to go. It was at this point that many once revered vestments were unstitched and cut up for other uses. There is for example a story that when Sir Walter Raleigh, a staunch Protestant in his Devon parish, was asked by a parishioner for the church's cope to be restored, he replied:

Yf it were not cut already for the sparmer (i.e. canopy) of a bed, you should have it.

Evidently, in 1563, Minsterworth church still had at least one vestment for there is a record from that year of the following letter being sent to the bishop:

> ... Richard Hoper and Elizabeth Hyet, church wardens, John Keylocke and Nicholas Heyward, parishioners, of Minsterworth present as follows. That the curate refuseth to weare a cope at the ministration of the Holy Communion and sayeth no man shall make him use any such or like superstition further on Sondayes. He doth wearie the parrishe with over longe preachinge both pystell and gospel, not being graduate or licensed otherwise.

Whether they were objecting more to the curate's refusal to wear the appropriate vestment for the Communion or to his long sermons is not clear, but they apparently were unhappy with him. Not all churchmen though held the same attitude as Minsterworth's curate and there were many rebels adhering to the old order prepared to die for their beliefs, some being hanged in their chasubles for their pains.

We can now only look at the embroidered remnant resting quietly in our local church and imagine what kind of encounters it might have had and how it survived for so long.

Survival and Recognition

Fast forward, if you will, around 400 years to 1953, the year when the second Queen Elizabeth ascended the throne. To celebrate her coronation, the Art Gallery & Museum in Cheltenham put on an exhibition of 'priceless treasures' from the Tudor period including paintings, furniture, tapestries and numerous examples of ecclesiastical artwork from that time. Item no.295 in the exhibition catalogue was a 'mutilated cope or chasuble (probably the latter)' which had been loaned to the exhibition by the church of St Peter's Minsterworth. After a brief description, the catalogue entry notes that:

> The vestment is supposed to have originally belonged to St Peter's Abbey Gloucester, and at the Dissolution to have been given to Minsterworth, where it was in 1563. The other half (sic) of this piece is in the possession of Winchcombe parish church.

Other sources also refer to the chasuble having belonged to the abbey in Gloucester but they all appear to stem from the aforementioned 1563 letter about the curate's refusal to wear a cope. Also there exists a letter sent from the bishop's palace in Gloucester to the Rev. Bartlett of Minsterworth in 1915 probably following a visit to the parish by the bishop. It too refers to the 1563 incident but the bishop stops

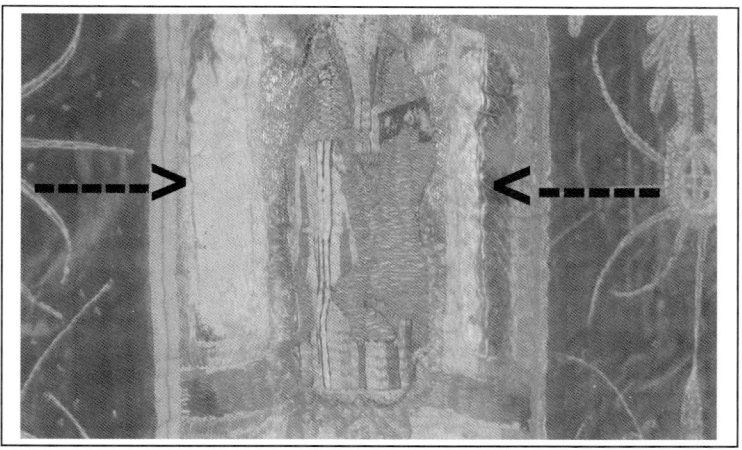

Areas of wear down to the base linen backcloth on one of the orphreys of the chasuble

short of associating the vestment with St Peter's abbey. All of this tends to raise the question: if the chasuble is the vestment referred to in 1563, was it just a slip of the tongue that those involved describe it as a 'cope'? In addition, if it did originally belong to the abbey in Gloucester, how does one explain the apparent connection with Winchcombe or possibly Hailes? One thing does however appear clear: parts of the orphrey band (the oldest part of the piece) had received considerable wear . This is evident from patches on one of the orphreys part way down the front of the garment where the embroidery has worn away right down to the linen backcloth; this quite likely is where the wearer's arms and hands would have rubbed on the fabric over many years.

Another strand needs to be explored however and that is Sir Richard Pate of Minsterworth. Although he is perhaps better known for his association with Cheltenham, Pate was a prominent Gloucestershire lawyer and rose to be both MP for, and Recorder of, Gloucester. In the 1540s he was appointed under-steward and keeper of the manorial courts of the dissolved abbeys of Cirencester and Hailes as well as guardian of the possessions of Deerhurst priory. He also acted as commissioner for inquiring into the chantries in Gloucestershire. In these capacities Pate, like so many others, must have been able to benefit from access to all 'these fruits ripe for the plucking'. It so happens that it was in 1566 that Pate purchased the lease of the manor and parsonage of Minsterworth where he possessed substantial premises and property. Before acquiring his grand house in Matson, Minsterworth was also for a time his family home. Is it more likely therefore that, rather than being a gift from Gloucester abbey, the chasuble found its way into Minsterworth through Richard Pate, possibly finding a safe home either with the resident vicar or another local person?

Up to this point, the garment may well have been complete still but at some later stage it was cut up and converted into the rectangular panel we see today, perhaps for use as a table cover or wall hanging. A potential clue as to when this happened is to be found with the material used as a border along the lower and side edges of the converted embroidery. Research into the particular material used suggests that it dates from the first half of the 17th century, i.e. some time after the Reformation. Intriguingly also, the research seems to indicate that the material originated from northern France.

Portrait of Sir Richard Pate (1516-88).(By kind permission of Cheltenham Art Gallery and Museum)

As far as the next 300 years of the embroidery's existence are concerned, the trail goes cold There is no evidence of recusant tendencies in Minsterworth to suggest that the embroidery may have been secretly kept by 'closet catholics' in the village. In September 1870, a report appeared in the Gloucester Journal of the consecration of the newly-built church which includes information on those features of the old church, like the pulpit and the font, that were retained in the new church. Significantly it makes no mention of the embroidery, although by 1886 the antiquarian Mary Ellen Bagnell-Oakley notes its presence in the parish. From the bishop's letter in 1915 we might conclude that it was then in the care of the vicar, and there is later correspondence to show that in 1929 it was Canon Bartlett who took the embroidery to the V & A Museum in London.

Following its return from the Museum, the vicar sent it to the Royal School of Needlework for treatment and it was there that the link with the Winchcombe panel was discovered. In 1930 Canon Bartlett (who claimed he had just spent £8..2s on the embroidery) noted that in that same year it had been exhibited at a Church Congress in Newport where 'it was much admired'. When he retired soon afterwards, he records handing the embroidery over to the churchwardens.

Our next encounter with the embroidery comes with an entry in " The King's England—Gloucestershire", edited by Arthur Mee and published in 1938, which briefly describes the antiquities of Minsterworth church , in particular the medieval embroidery which it describes as half of a 'precious' 14th century cope. Coincidentally, soon after this the Rev Brockwell arrived in the parish and the August 1939 issue of St Peter's parish magazine contains the following note:

> During the long vacancy, Mr A Phelps took charge of what is perhaps
> our greatest art treasure, the famous Minsterworth portion of a fourteenth
> century cope. We shall have to decide how best to preserve and exhibit
> this treasure……
>
>   Your sincere friend'
>   C A B Brockwell

(Mr Arthur Phelps of Brook Farm in Oakle Street was a churchwarden at the time)

This note by the vicar is the first indication that anyone locally thought seriously that the embroidery was worth displaying in the church, although this step may not actually have been taken until the early 1950s. This is suggested by the small plaque fixed to the bottom of the display case in the church which houses the embroidery. After describing the supposed origins of the embroidery, the plaque states:

> … This case was given by his wife in memory of Ernest Wallace Smart,
> lay-reader of this parish, who died aged 69 on 1st January 1955.

For posterity?

In 2009, the church became concerned about the deteriorating condition of the embroidery and initiated a project to have it professionally conserved and remounted. The purpose of this was not just to halt the deterioration but also to preserve this precious possession for the benefit of future generations of church-goers and visitors to the church. Recognising the importance of this aim, the church's Parochial Church Council in 2009 resolved that the embroidery should remain in the church permanently and never ever be disposed of. It is remarkable that this ancient artefact has held on tenaciously to survival for the best part of half a millennium, thanks to having been so well cared for by successive generations of Minsterworth church people. We at least owe it to them that it endures as a reminder of our church's, and nation's, eventful past.

IV.
LAMENTABLE HAPPENINGS

There cannot be a single village in the country that has not, at some time or other, been afflicted by calamities or tragedies. As history shows, Minsterworth is certainly no exception. Everyone knows of the regular floods which the river Severn has inflicted on our village over time. These have come to be regarded as a seasonal hazard but often they bring destruction, hardship and sometimes tragedy. Records of flooding around Minsterworth exist from at least the 17th century. In 1606/7 there occurred a "Great Flood" which affected the whole of the Severn estuary from at least Somerset up to Gloucester, resulting in many hundreds of men, women and children perishing. (Some maintain that this was caused by a tsunami event originating out at sea but this has yet to be firmly established.) We do not have any records of how this flood affected Minsterworth but there is information from other local sources which may help. The Berkeley Castle papers relating to this event contain a quotation from the Gentleman's Magazine for 1762 stating how:

> ….all the country from Bristol to Gloucester, on both sides of the Severne, was overflowed to the distance of six miles.

The same papers also include a statement that:

> This flood is affirmed by tradition to have risen nearly as high as Frampton

The event was also recorded in Arlingham where, according to an entry in the parish records for 20th January 1606/7, there was:

> ...an exceeding great fludde.

An extraordinary flood also occurred in November 1770 when, according to St Peter's church records, three men of the village and a fourth "stranger" were drowned in Minsterworth Ham. This too was when flood water entered the old parish church and saturated everything in the parish chest. The effect of this flood hereabouts is also found in notes written by the then vicar of Elmore concerning the effects of the flooding around Elmore Back (parts of which at that time were in

Minsterworth parish): He writes that:

> On Saturday ye 17th of 9ber the Severn was greatly Swelled by a very heavy Rain, which being stopped by the Tide, ran clear over the Sea Walls above two Miles in length in this parish, and Occasion'd the most frightful Inundation that ever was known here by any man living……. Some in boats leading Beasts half drowned out of their once dry Grounds; Others picking up their household goods which were now afloat & going away…..Almost all the Cyder both old and new was damaged, the hoarded Apples carried away, the clean wheat in the Bags wetted, the Cheese on the lofts, and the butter in the Dairy [spoiled] and the Corn and Hay ricks up to the eaves in Water…. There was happily no lives lost.

Next, in 1852, flood water entered St Peter's church in Minsterworth filling the nave to a depth of 18 inches. It was this misfortune that eventually led to a decision, ten years or so later, to pull down the old medieval church and rebuild it at a higher level on the old foundations. A dedicatory stone plaque describing all this can be seen on the north wall of the chancel.

A contemporary woodcut of the effects of the 1606/07 flooding in Somerset. Even allowing for artistic licence, it shows how terrible the consequences of that event must have been at least in that part of the country.

A number of exceptional floods have occurred since then, notably in 1947, 1960 and again in 2007, each bringing its hardships to the local community. In 1947, Mrs Christabel Mortimer lived in Street End Cottage and this is how she described conditions then:

> When the Tuffeyhayes bank broke and we could hear the water rushing down through Calcotts Green and Fred Boyce came to my Dad to get the cattle out of the orchard into the shed. So Harold Boyce stayed in the

(continued overleaf)

house with me at Street End and Fred Boyce and my Dad went to get the Viner-Ellis cattle on to higher ground down the other side at the back of the church. When they came back for us they couldn't get along the lane, the water was so deep so they had to come along the river bank, down the Black Drive in through over by the coal shed and Harold and I went and we had to walk back down the bank with water either side of us and we got down by the church and back up to Granny Phelps at Lyn Paddock. And in the morning they got the boat out and sailed all the way up to Calcotts Green. And they got over to my Granny Webb at Snowdrop Cottage—the water was in the cottage but she had got on to the table and they carried her out and got her in a boat and they took her to Street End Cottage where our old cat Pimple was sitting on top of the well!

Fire has also afflicted the village more than once. In May 1702, the medieval church's steeple was totally destroyed by lightning. Details of this event are contained in manuscript notes on the history of Newent dated 1707 which record that:

On Thursday May 7th 1702 about 4 of ye clock in ye afternoon there happened such a violent & horrible Lightning and Thunder at Minsterswrth church yt a ball of fire as bigg as a Bushell was seen to fall upon its wooden steeple, which burnt it down & melted the 5 bells. which hung in the Tower, doing great Damage thereunto.

A year later however, the churchwardens were able to report the good news that the steeple was to be repaired and in 1788 a new peal of 6 bells was given by the lord of the manor Sir Charles Barrow of Hygrove.

One dramatic conflagration to hit Minsterworth is all the more striking perhaps because it occurred in modern times, well within living memory for some. The fire rendered one family homeless virtually within minutes and destroyed the whole of their home and its contents. The Gloucester Journal of 17th January 1942 contained a report that shortly after 4 a.m., Mr C W Browning of Pool End Cottage situated near the river bank was awakened by his wife because she had heard unusual noises downstairs. Looking from the bedroom window, Mr Browning saw the reflection of flames on the river bank. He was able to lead his three young sons to safety but by this time the flames had cut off escape by means of the staircase and Mr Browning had to lower his wife from the bedroom by means of a sheet and then escaped himself by jumping to safety. One of Mr Browning's sons was dispatched to run barefooted to the vicarage where a telephone call was made to P.C. (Hector) Evans, the village "bobby", who in turn called the Gloucester Fire Brigade. They arrived quite swiftly but their water pump failed to work and a new one had to be sent for. By the time it arrived the fire had gained a firm hold of the cottage and its roof had collapsed. No-one had time to collect any belongings which were totally destroyed.

All that was left of the kitchen following the fire at Pool End Cottage. (Courtesy of the Gloucester Journal)

The ruin of Pool End cottage (popularly believed to have once been a river-side ale and cider house called the Ship Inn) still stands beside the river just upstream from the Naight and the son who ran to the vicarage for help was John Browning who is still among us today (but living now in Birdwood). John remembers the event well and recounts how much the family were supported in the village. In particular, Mrs Vyner Ellis of Minsterworth Court stepped in and offered temporary accommodation for the Browning family in the rear half of the old Cray Croft cottage.

Mr Browning with his three sons. John is on the far right. (Courtesy of the Gloucester Journal)

There is no getting away from the fact that life in the past was fragile and precarious for most ordinary people. In his recent book *A Short History of Private Life,* Bill Bryson writes that:

> .... in the 15th and 16th centuries the chances of an early death were high. The average marriage lasted just ten years before one or the other of the partners expired.

Reliable church records for St Peter's church are available only from the 17th century but they certainly reflect a relatively high death rate notably among women at or soon after childbirth and of infants and young children. Typical of such entries in the registers of baptisms, marriages and burials are those relating to the Hayward family of Minsterworth towards the end of the 1600s.

In November 1679 Joan, wife of John Hayward was buried and barely six months later probably this same John Hayward, widower, married a second time to Ann Tovey, "spincer". Ten years later, on 9th July 1690, the baptism is recorded of Thomas, the son of John Hayward and his wife Ann but this is quickly followed on 11 July 1690 by the burial of Ann and on 25 July 1690 by the burial of Thomas the infant son of John Hayward (no mention of Ann). Seemingly undeterred by these set-backs, in November 1690, apparently the same John Hayward is registered as marrying a Sibble Kempe of Churcham.

War also brings tragedy. We cannot begin to know what disasters or tragedies might have been inflicted on Minsterworth by the conflicts of past centuries: invading Romans, marauding Vikings, rapacious Normans or even the Civil War campaigns around besieged Gloucester in the 17th century (when Westbury on Severn and Highnam were certainly scenes of warfare). There have also been plenty of wars fought abroad in which Minsterworth men may have been required to risk their lives for king and country. The 1522 Military Survey for Gloucestershire lists around 70 men in Minsterworth capable of serving in the king's army and, about a hundred years later in 1608, John Smith's Men and Armour survey lists 120 male inhabitants in the parish deemed capable of bearing arms for the king. How many of these men, if any, were actually called to arms and possibly lost their lives in hostilities in England or abroad is unknown.

For reliable facts, we have to come up to the 20th century and in particular to the two World Wars in which this country was involved. No-one can contemplate the memorials in St Peter's church and churchyard without being struck by the losses suffered by the Selwyn families of Minsterworth. In the Great War of 1914-18, two of their boys were killed and in the 1939-45 war three made the final sacrifice. The Selwyns were a large extended family and it seems that none of these boys were closer than cousins to each other. Even so, such a scale of losses affecting two successive generations in the family must have been appalling for all involved.

More poignant still is the tragedy conveyed by a tiny memorial in the churchyard and a simple plaque inside the church on the north wall. The sad little gravestone refers simply to Jennifer and Annabel Viner-Brady aged 8 and 4 and a plaque in the church enlarges on this by stating that they were both "killed by enemy action". It appears that the two little girls were taken by their mother from London to Exeter in 1942 in order to avoid the bombings taking place in the capital. In March 1942, the RAF had carried out a massive bombing raid on the German city of Lubeck. An outraged German leadership decided to carry out retaliatory raids on selected cities in England which came to be known as the "Baedeker" raids, since the cities chosen for attack were reputedly selected from among those awarded three stars in the German Baedeker Tourist Guide to Britain. These included York, Norwich Canterbury, Bath and …. the ancient city of Exeter.

Grave stone to Jennifer Elizabeth and Annabel Viner-Brady in St Peter's churchyard, Minsterworth

The Baedeker raids on Exeter took place on two days in April and again on 3 and 4 May 1942. In all, 1500 houses in the city were totally destroyed and 265 persons were killed and many more injured. In the 4 May raid, a house at 24 West Avenue received a direct hit as a result of which six persons were killed. Among the dead were little Jennifer and Annabel and it is said that their mother (Molly Viner-Brady) spent two days trapped in the ruins with her two dead daughters beside her. Many of the dead were buried in a mass grave in Exeter but not the two girls who were brought back to Minsterworth for burial beside their Viner-Ellis ancestors.

We cannot conceive of the numberless unknown or unforgotten misfortunes and tragedies to have happened in the village. Even so, basic factual details from the past, such as those above, speak strongly to us of the human condition and of the adverse experiences of our Minsterworth predecessors.

V.
HELLFIRE JACK
(A Tale of Fame and Family Ties)

One of the most popular music hall entertainers in late Edwardian England was a singer and comedian Billy Williams. He was best known for his 'chorus songs', one of his most successful hits being 'When Father Papered the Parlour'. He worked closely with the song writer Fred Godfrey who, in his lifetime, wrote over 900 songs including such Great War favourites as 'Take Me back to Dear Old Blighty' and 'Bless 'Em All'. Both men enjoyed betting on the horses and, in 1913, they combined to produce a highly popular song entitled 'Jean Loves All The Jockeys'. The chorus of this song was effectively a complete roll call of all the most famous jockeys of the day. Unless you are a keen fan of 'Sport of Kings' history, it is unlikely that these names will mean anything today but, among the jockeys named in the song's chorus was one Charlie Trigg. Earlier, in 1906, the Ogdens cigarette manufacturers had issued a new set of cigarette cards about race horse owners and jockeys and among the titles in the set was one 'C Trigg'. All this is the more notable given that Charlie Trigg is one of Gloucester's, and Minsterworth's, largely unsung sporting heroes from the past.

Charlie Trigg—the jockey (taken in 1904)

Charlie Trigg—the man

Charlie Trigg certainly appears to have been quite special. In 1903, after being a riding apprentice for only a short time, he won at Sandown Park on Pretty Polly and went on from there to become one of the leading flat racers of the day and a national sporting hero. His fearless riding style earned him the nickname 'Hellfire Jack'. He is reputed to have ridden five consecutive winners in one day at Edinburgh and, for his win on Copper King in the first ever meet at Newbury in 1905, he received a valuable gold-mounted whip. For a time he was associated with the prestigious Manton stable and rode for a variety of prominent horse-owners including the Rothschilds in Switzerland. He is recorded as having ridden winners abroad in Ireland, France and Austria and his fame on the turf also reached the Antipodes, where articles about him appeared in both Adelaide and Hobart newspapers of the day. In the Hobart 'Daily Mercury' of July 29 1911, Charlie is asked which was the greatest horse he ever rode:

> Without a moment's hesitation he replied, 'Pretty Polly. I was the first to ride Pretty Polly in public, being only a boy then. I think she won that race by about a furlong. Her action was magnificent. I had only to sit there and let her go … I never wish to ride a better.

Probably however his greatest success was in the 1910 Epsom Oaks classic which he won on the 3 year old filly Rosedrop, coming in at 7-1. But 1911 has to be his best year during which he rode 111 winners and secured for himself second place in the national list of winning jockeys for that year. In his racing career over 17 years, Charlie rode over 7,000 mounts, won 843 races, rode 770 "seconds" and 883 "thirds". His last win was in 1918 at Catterick Bridge on a horse called Frenzy and soon afterwards, at the age of 37, he retired from racing on account of increasing deafness.

According to his birth certificate, Charles George Trigg was born in Chaxhill on 9th January 1881. His mother was Ellen Trigg, one of four daughters of William and Rhoda Trigg whose family lived in The White House at Dinny. It appears that, for the birth, Ellen (described as a 'domestic servant') went to stay with her sister Caroline who at that time lived with her husband William Greening at Cyprus Cottage, just down the road at Walmore Hill. The birth certificate provides no information about Charlie's father whose identity remains a mystery. Caroline and William Greening subsequently moved to the Trigg family home at The White House and it is there that Charlie seems to have spent his early years.

As a boy, he showed great interest in ponies and horses belonging to neighbouring farmers. It is not known when he decided to work with race horses but, by 1903 in his very early twenties, he was already riding in major races, after having been an apprentice boy 'just a short time back'. (Horse racing seems to have run through the whole family since at least two later Greening boys also turned out to be jockeys , notably Derrick (Mick) Greening (born c.1921) who raced between 1939 and 1974.

Heavy shouldered, with dark eyebrows, Charlie is said to have been a rough type in his early years. His rural Gloucestershire origins can be detected in one story told of him. When riding Pretty Polly in 1903, his horse suddenly pulled up ten lengths in front of the field, which included his jockey friend George Thursby, whereupon Charlie called out to Thursby:

> "If you'd 'a caught I'se, you'd 'a beaten I'se, because I'se was all out!"

It was not long however before he was taught to dress well and to vie with his brother jockeys in the grace of his profession.

In spite of his peripatetic and exciting life as a jockey, he always stayed in touch with his roots at The White House and with the rest of his family in Minsterworth. One of his mother's other sisters was Alice Trigg, She suffered from severe deafness (a family trait perhaps) and her daughter Joan Gardner of Birdwood remembers how Charlie paid for his aunt Alice to have treatment for her hearing problem. He also used to invite Alice to stay with him in London and together they would go to the theatre. There is a picture postcard that Charlie sent to a 'Miss A Trigg' (probably his aunt Alice) from Brighton in August 1906 . The picture shows two dapperly dressed young men; one is Charlie and the other probably his friend and fellow jockey W (Walter or William) Griggs. His short note on the reverse reads:

> Dear Alice. Just a few lines hoping this will find you in the very best of good health. And what do you think of Mr Griggs and myself. Writing soon. With love and best wishes.

Charlie must have felt as if he was on the crest of a wave in life and then, to cap it all, he met and fell for a young lady. She was Winifred Rhoda Maynard Davis, the daughter of a London bank manager. And thus it was, on 30th March 1907, Charlie and Winifred exchanged marriage vows at St Andrew's Church Westminster, with Charlie's friend Mr Griggs very likely acting as best man. The happy couple settled in Dulwich and the marriage was in due course blessed by the birth in or around 1910 of a girl they called Phyllis.

A picture of Charlie Trigg and his friend and fellow jockey W Griggs taken around 1906.

Inevitably, there were some who observed that Winifred had married beneath herself but all seemed to go well. Charlie's star in the racing firmament continued to shine brightly and it was only his deafness (we are told) that caused him to retire from riding in 1918. What could go wrong?

A portrait of Winifred Trigg (photograph by courtesy of Keith Pearson, Winifred's grandson).

In time though, the marriage went wrong. Such was Charlie's fame that we can read all about it in The Times newspaper of May 1st 1919. Under the headline 'A Jockey's Divorce Suit: Trigg v. Trigg and Kippax', the report indicates that Charles George Trigg was petitioning for the dissolution of his marriage with Winifred Rhoda Maynard Trigg on the grounds of her adultery with Captain Percy Walter Kippax. It goes on:

> …...In 1915 or 1916 the respondent's manner changed; she was drinking more than was good for her and she tried to irritate him. On one or two occasions he gave her a smack for it, and she got a solicitor to write a letter to him. Nothing came of that, and they continued to live together. In 1918 her manner changed completely and she refused to have anything to do with him., He was constantly away racing, and the respondent was left alone a good deal. On January 1st last he received a letter from his wife's solicitor saying that she had decided to leave him owing to his treatment of her. He wrote denying that there had been any ill treatment….. Evidence was given that the co-respondent had frequently visited the respondent in the petitioner's absence, and had made his escape through the hedge when the petitioner came home; and that they had stayed together in October, November and December 1918 at the Harbour Hotel, Lowestoft.
> Mr Justice Coleridge pronounced a decree nisi, with costs and the custody of the child'

Some have attributed the problem with the fact that Charlie was in Switzerland, riding for the Rothschild family, when war broke out, during which time the relationship broke down. However one reads the situation, the judge himself appears to have accepted that Charlie was the aggrieved party, and this is reinforced by his being awarded costs and, importantly, the custody of young Phyllis, then barely 9 or 10 years old. Only those who personally knew Charlie at this point can assess how all this affected him, but it was clearly a low point in his life.

A portrait of little Phyllis, aged approx. 12 months. (Photograph by courtesy of Keith Pearson.)

Phyllis came to Minsterworth to stay temporarily with the family at The White House, but this became her permanent home and, so it is said, Charlie paid for an extension to the house to help with the additional resident. She continued her schooling at Denmark Road High School and afterwards found work in the local telephone exchange. Phyllis was a keen Girl Guide and it was at a Guider function organised by Mrs Margery Lane at Appithorne in Minsterworth that she met Margery's brother, Peter Pearson, a young theological student. Eventually, Mr Pearson became ordained, he and Phyllis married and for a time they lived at Appithorne. Of their three children, two (Keith and Rachel) now live in the United States, but Keith regularly visits England and keeps in close touch with his family roots, including those in Minsterworth. Charlie's ex-wife may have re-married. She certainly had another child since both Keith and Rachel vaguely remember once meeting their grandmother Winifred and a son called Douglas Maynard, evidently Phyllis's half-brother.

People who knew him personally say that, after the divorce, Charlie lost much of his interest in life. His biography published in the Bloodstock Breeders' Review for 1945 states that, after his retirement from racing, he came to live at The White House; also that he had lost most of his money through a 'domestic transaction' and his attempt at pig-farming met with only moderate success. It is said that at

An early view of the White House before its modernisation and showing, on the right, the extension which supposedly Charlie Trigg helped have erected. The present occupants Mr and Mrs Roger Jayne have direct links with the Greening and Trigg families.

some point The White House was in danger of being lost to the bank, a fate avoided only by Charlie's cousin Mary (Polly) Greening buying the house from him. He eventually moved to Gloucester, for a time living in lodgings in St Mary's Square near the Cathedral. There are still local folk who remember how he would walk or bus from Gloucester to Minsterworth to visit his family and friends here. He is described as always being well-dressed in a suit and bowler hat and with a flower in his lapel. He invariably had a cheery word for those he met, often expressing his cheeky sense of humour by asking "Can you lend us a bob?" Another reason for his visits to the village was to bring his laundry to be washed by Mrs Catherine Twigg at Bodnams Cottage who took in washing from 'the big houses' round about.

And so life passed by for Charlie until late 1945 when, at 65 years of age, he contracted pneumonia and died in Gloucester General Hospital. The Times newspaper of 31st December 1945 carried a short report of his death, referring to him as 'the well-known jockey' and recounting some of his successes on the turf. But it was to his family roots that Charlie finally returned. He was brought from the hospital to Minsterworth and buried in St Peter's churchyard on 29 December 1945. The funeral was arranged by the local undertaker Mr Albert (Bert) Prosser and the bill for it came to £24. 12s. 0p. The account was settled by the Rev Peter Pearson, Phyllis's husband and Charlie's son-in-law.

VI.

WHY SHOULD THE DEVIL HAVE ALL THE GOOD TUNES?

Calcott's Green on the south side of Minsterworth is a collection of pretty cottages looking out over the fields and orchards towards the River Severn. It is a tranquil place and, apart from the occasional car or farm tractor, there is little to hear but the lowing of cows from Eric Watkin's Elms Farm or the cry of a startled pheasant. There was a time though when a passer-by, walking along the Street there at a certain time on a Sunday morning, would also have heard drifting on the air the sounds of lusty hymn singing. It would have been emanating from the Wesleyan Methodist chapel which, for well over a century had occupied a spot on the rising ground just behind the cottages.

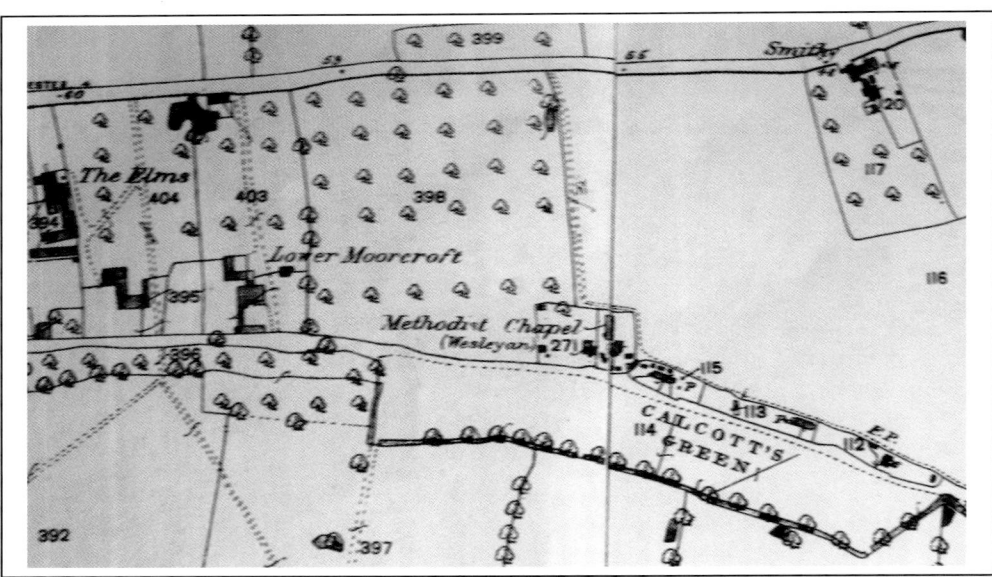

Detail from the 1881 Ordnance Survey map showing the position of the Methodist Chapel in Minsterworth. The main A48 road is running along the top of the picture.

The chapel building was erected in 1845 and it served Minsterworth folk continuously from then until the 1970s when, in a structurally poor state and with a dwindling number of worshippers, the chapel, the land on which it stood and the neighbouring Chapel House were sold off by the Methodist Church . Today, a keen observer might spot the name 'Chapel Cottage' claimed by one of the houses there but, of the chapel itself, there is nothing to show it ever existed.

How did the chapel come to this small corner of Gloucestershire? And what mark did it make on the village and its people? It is worth looking at, not least because the initial stirrings of the Methodist movement owed much to a very special Gloucester man.

Looking back from our standpoint in the 21st century, it is difficult to appreciate just how important religion has been in the daily lives of most ordinary people in the past and to understand the intensity of feelings that were aroused about how a Christian life should be led. Sometimes this led to disputes between the different factions and even riots and violence. Over the few centuries following the Reformation and the establishment of the Church of England, new 'protestant' groups began to develop generally known as Dissenters or Nonconformists. Successors to the earlier Puritan movement, these included Presbyterians, Baptists, Congregationalists and Unitarians, all fervently wishing not to conform to the precepts of the Church of England with which they had become disillusioned.

The first half of the 18th century also saw the beginning of the industrial revolution and what was to become a massive change in the country as large numbers of impoverished working people moved away from the land into the burgeoning new industrial centres seeking new employment in the textile mills, engineering factories and mines. Living conditions in these new towns were often horrendous, creating pressing social problems that neither the government nor the established church could deal with.

This then was the setting for the 'Great Awakening' of Methodist evangelical fervour which, by the middle of the 18th century, was to work a major change throughout English society. At the time, the various dissenting denominations, like the Methodists, each fervently held on to their individual differences, but all had one thing in common: in those times of great social upheaval, they fulfilled peoples' needs by providing them with spiritual support and membership of a stable and reliable community.

The Preachers

The story, if I may call it that, starts with George Whitefield who was born in 1714 at the Bell Inn in Southgate Street Gloucester where his father was the licensee. He attended the King's School and later the Crypt School, showing no particular academic ability but demonstrating an ability as a speaker and actor (as a boy at school he regularly made 'speeches' before the Mayor and City Congregation). On leaving school he became pot boy at the Bell Inn, cleaning the rooms, but with the help of wealthier relatives he soon found his way to Oxford where, in 1732, he matriculated. It was at Oxford that he met John and Charles Wesley and in 1735 he joined their Christian society of students (the so-called 'Holy Club') whose members were referred to as 'Methodists'. When he began preaching, people saw that he was not only a preacher, but a born orator and his sermons often had the effect of making hearers go 'quite mad' with religious fervour. He was ordained in Gloucester Cathedral in 1736 but, because of his connection with the Dissenters and style of preaching, his fellow clergy refused to allow him to preach in their churches. His response was to begin preaching in the open air where he could be heard by large numbers of people. He had the misfortune to have a distinct cast in his eye (the result of a childhood measles attack) but this seems not to have affected his charisma and he went on to gain a massive religious following both in this country and in North America, which he visited frequently. He preached several times in Gloucester between 1730 and 1741. He died in America in 1777 after reputedly having preached as many as 18,000 sermons to an estimated 10 million people.

George Whitefield, preacher and evangeliser (1714-1777)

Above all though, the Methodist movement is most closely associated with the brothers John and Charles Wesley. John was born in 1703 and Charles in 1707, both in the small Lincolnshire town of Epworth where their father was rector. In 1726, John became a fellow of Lincoln College Oxford where, with George Whitfield and others, he organised the 'Holy Club' devoting themselves to religious duties and visiting the sick and prisoners. Following periods first as a missionary to American natives in Georgia and then on visits to Germany, he began his life-long vocation of preaching and organising the growth of numerous local Methodist societies around the country. A powerful orator like Whitefield, he preached a doctrine of striving for Christian perfection, faith through self-denial and care for the poor and needy. Out of the Methodist movement also came the establishment of the Sunday School system, which was set up by another Gloucester man named Robert Raikes.

Methodism appealed mostly to the lower and industrial classes but also to many of the middle and upper classes. Among the latter was the Countess of Huntingdon who responded to the call by founding the 'Countess of Huntingdon's Connexion' which set up numerous Methodist chapels throughout the country. More locally, the cause was also taken up by Mrs Catherine Boevey of Flaxley Abbey who invited local poor children to dine at her house on Sundays and afterwards taught them.

John Wesley, Evangeliser and Preacher (1703-1791)

John Wesley first preached in Gloucester in 1730 and frequently from 1739 onwards. In 1786, he gave what was described as a 'fiery' sermon at St Bartholomew's Hospital and another in the 'Tollbooth' (probably the old Boothall). At first, Methodists in Gloucester met in one another's houses but around 1770 they moved to a newly-registered meeting place in Cobbler's Hall (on the present-day Kimbrose Triangle) and then, in 1787 to a newly built chapel in lower Northgate Street (once located opposite Worcester Street but now demolished). For many years, this was to be the centre for the local Methodist circuit.

Notionally at least, John Wesley remained an Anglican churchman throughout but, like Whitefield, he was not made welcome by the established church and he and his fellow Methodists frequently encountered public opposition and even mob violence. In his journal for 3rd March 1743, Wesley gives a lurid account of a trial at the Gloucester Assizes when residents of probably Minchinhampton were accused of mobbing and abusing Methodists, citing that:

> …. for about ten months last past it has prevailed very much in Glocestershire, especially at Hampton where Mr Adams has a dwelling house and has been much blessed to many people. This displeased the grand enemy of souls who stirred up many of the baser sort, privately encouraged by some of a higher rank, to come from time to time in great numbers with a lowbell [a bell once used to scare birds at night] and horn to beset the house and berate and abuse the people….. They put Mr Adams and Mr Williams into the skin-pit [? a tannery bath] and brook….. [The mob] broke into Mr Adams' house one Saturday night at 11 o'clock when there was no preaching, made those that were in bed get up, and searched the oven, cellar and every corner of the house to see whether they could find any Methodists.

We are told that the jury found all the defendants guilty. Somewhat later, on 5 June 1769, the Gloucester Journal reported that:

> On Saturday morning a Methodist preacher, who had disturbed the peace of this city with his enthusiastic rant, was flogged through the streets by order of the mayor.

But unquestionably, John Wesley is above all remembered for his exhaustive preaching tours covering the length and breadth of the whole country including Ireland, always gaining new converts and setting up local meeting houses and chapels. He travelled at least forty-five hundred miles every year, mostly on horseback and not without a good deal of hardship. His travels and the kind of reception he received from local people are copiously recorded in his personal journals. A typical entry is this one concerning a visit to Gloucestershire in the late 1700s:

> Tuesday, 18 [March 1788]. I preached in Painswick at ten. Here we also wanted room for the audience; and all were still as night. At six in the evening I began at Gloucester …. High and low, rich and poor, flock together, and seem to devour the word … Many, I believe, were cut to the heart.

Still in this part of the country is a journal entry in March 1756 concerning his journey from Bristol to Brecon via Coleford:

> [From Pill] I rode to the Old Passage [i.e. Aust-Beachley] but finding we could not pass we went on to Purton which we reached at four in the

(continued overleaf)

> afternoon. But we were no nearer still for the boatmen lived on the other side and the wind was so high we could not possibly make them hear. However, we determined to wait a while and in a quarter of an hour they came of their own accord. We reached Coleford before seven and found a plain, loving people who received the word of God with gladness.

In February of 1747, John was travelling north to take over from his brother Charles and his journal vividly describes the conditions in which the journey was made, as the following extracts show:

> ....The wind turned full north, and blew so exceeding hard and keen, that when we came to Hatfield, neither my companions nor I had much use of our hands and feet. …… In Baldock-field the storm began in earnest. The large hail drove so vehemently in our faces, that we could not see, nor hardly breath…. [After Bugden] we pushed on and were met in the middle of an open field with so violent a storm of rain and hail as we had not before. It drove through our coats, great and small, boots and everything, and yet froze as it fell, even upon our eyebrows…… [After Stilton] Here a new difficulty arose , from the snow lying in large drifts. Sometimes horse and man were well nigh swallowed up. Yet in less than an hour we were brought safe to Stamford.

It has been said that during the 52 years of his ministry, John Wesley travelled about 4,000 miles a year and preached more than 40,000 sermons.

The need for a form of organisation was seen early on and, in 1744, there took place the first annual national conference of Methodists at which a scheme of administration was established to support the work of evangelising and pastoral care around the country. Soon afterwards, circuits were formed and preaching houses were set up served by travelling preachers and part-time local preachers. At one such conference in 1779, three full-time ministers were appointed to Gloucestershire. After John Wesley's death in1791, Methodists found themselves increasingly at odds with the established church and within a few years the 'Society of Methodists' formally broke away from the Church of England.

Of course no account of the Methodist movement would be complete without reference to John Wesley's brother Charles Wesley (1707-1788). At Oxford he was seen as a rather frivolous young man but he eventually succumbed to his brother's attempts to make him more serious and, in 1735, he was ordained a deacon of the

Church of England and then priest. He may not have had the dynamism of his brother and he believed less in striving for perfection before death (as his brother did), more in a gradual growth in holiness. Even so, he committed himself fully to the same work of evangelising and preaching all round the country and, by the 1750s, he was writing the hymns for which he is now famously known. His output was prodigious and even more remarkable when we are told that many were composed on his travels, on horseback and in shorthand! He meant his hymns to be highly sing-able and it has been said that he was even happy to have them sung to secular song tunes popular in pubs and music halls at the time. Hence came the saying, associated especially with the Methodists, 'Why should the Devil have all the good tunes?'.

Charles' hymns were his greatest gift to Methodism and they now feature in hymn books used by different Christian denominations the world over. Whether you are a serious churchgoer or not, Wesley's hymns will be stirring stuff to sing wherever you encounter them. The music for 'Hark the Herald Angels Sing' as sung today may have come from the hand of Mendelssohn, but how many Christmas carol singers today realise that the lyrics they sing are Charles Wesley's. His version actually started 'Hark How All the Welkins [Heavens] Ring' but this was amended by none other than George Whitefield.

The Methodists come to Minsterworth

The people of Minsterworth during the 18th century must have heard of, if not actually heard, John or Charles Wesley when they were in Gloucestershire but, if Methodism made any impression on them, we have no record of it. By the early 19th century however, improved social conditions saw an increase in churchgoing generally and further expansion within the Methodist movement. A chapel was built in Cheltenham as early as 1812 and between the 1820s and 1840s numerous additional chapels and meeting places started up in Gloucester and its environs. The 'Old Chapel' in Westbury-on-Severn was built in 1836. The centenary of the Methodist movement in 1839 provided still more impetus to the building of chapels all around the country. This though was a period of schism and controversy within the movement from which emerged a strong desire for reform in the Methodist church movements. Particular controversy arose in Gloucester in 1849 following the expulsion of three reforming ministers from the Wesleyan Methodist Conference of that year and, in 1850, a band of reformers resolved to break away; founding their own chapels in the city and appointing their own ministers. This society, so we are told, also had members in Hartpury, Hucclecote, Churchdown and Minsterworth.

Slightly before this, in 1834, the bishop of Gloucester was notified that a 'certain dwelling house situate at Over' and occupied by William Preen, 'labourer' in the parish of Minsterworth, was being used as a place of religious worship by Protestant Dissenters. We hear nothing more of this site but a few years later, in 1838, a similar notification was sent to the bishop by William Viner-Ellis of Minsterworth to the effect that a dwelling house occupied by a Mary Hawkins in Minsterworth was to be used as a place of worship by dissenters. We can't be sure about the identity of this Mary Hawkins, but it seems likely that the house she lived in sat on a plot of land called 'Littles' which ran down to The Street at Calcotts Green and on which stood a cottage occupied by two families. In 1845, this same piece of land was purchased by 'Richard Stephens and Other Trustees of the Wesleyan Methodist Society' for the purposes of building a new chapel, which was erected that same year. The cottage in question was almost certainly that which later became known as 'Old Chapel House'.

From old photographs, we know that the chapel was a sturdy-looking plain brick building with its entrance façade looking north towards the main road. Inside, there was a main floor with a gallery above and a door at the far end leading to a separate schoolroom; an undercroft contained room for tables, chairs and a kitchen. It was here that successive generations of Minsterworth families worshipped every Sunday, sent their children to Sunday school and Scouts, and held their various social events. The first years of the chapel were not all plain sailing however. Perhaps it was related to the reform controversy within the Methodist church generally at the time but, in 1851, a number of the members of the Minsterworth Methodist community left the chapel to meet in a reformers' preaching room in a building at The Naight, occupied by a Richard Clifford (possibly the same Richard Clifford who, in the 1851 census for Minsterworth, is described as a 58 year old labourer). The leader of this break-away group was non-other than Richard Stephens who had led in the setting up of the chapel only six years earlier. Reading the 4 January 1851 Gloucester Journal article about the affair, it would appear that the cause of the trouble was an attempt by the local circuit preachers to disown Mr Stephens and several others for going to worship at a different meeting in Gloucester. This action seems to have been against the wishes of the majority of the chapel's supporters since the average attendance at The Naight in that particular year at its three

Sunday meetings was 51, compared to less than seven at the chapel (which had seats for at least 80 people). Fortunately, the schism appears to have been short-lived and the Stephens' family remained closely linked with the chapel for many more years and the small grave yard at the chapel once contained the Stephens' family vault.

For many years the Hurcombe family served as caretakers for the chapel and Walter Hurcombe (now in his eighties and living in Robinswood) recalls his grandparents and then his parents performing this duty. His mother also played the organ in the chapel. For quite a time, by virtue of their being the caretakers, the Hurcombes had occupied one half of the 'Old Chapel House' and, in 1960, Walter moved into the other half with his young family. Walter describes how, as a youngster, he had to tend the chapel's small grave yard, including the Stephens family vault.

'Old Chapel House' in Calcotts Green photographed in the early 1900s, showing members of the Hurcombe family who then lived in one half of the house. On the left, behind the house, can be seen the rear of the Wesleyan Chapel. Today the house, much altered, is known as 'Chapel Cottage'.

Other local families attending the chapel in later times included the Moggs, Cliffords and Butts and the names of Elsie Boyce, Miss Annie Stephens (the chapel's Sunday school teacher) and Joanne Stait have also been recorded. Up until the 1920s, the only access to the chapel was by footpaths: one from the main road, another up from The Street and a third that ran from the eastern end of Calcott's Green along the bank behind the cottages. With the advent of the motorcar however this was obviously inadequate and in 1928 a proper driveway from the main road to the chapel was installed. The land for this was sold to the chapel by Mr Child of Eame Hill and there is an old photograph of 'Chapel Road' being formally opened by Mrs Vyner Ellis . The wooden gate at the main road end of the drive was donated by Mr Charlie Mogg and until recently it still carried a sign saying 'to Minsterworth Methodist Chapel'. Today the driveway leads to a modern house called 'Chapel House'.

It is almost certain that this tea party took place in the garden at the rear of Oakle House, Oakle Street, the home of Mr John Clifford Stephens. It is likely that the bearded gentlemen (front right) is actually Mr Stephens himself. His family's close connection with the Wesleyan Chapel in Minsterworth makes it possible that this was a chapel tea party. We cannot be sure about the date but the style of dress suggests around 1910. John Stephens and his second wife Mary (nee Messenger) are buried together in Minsterworth churchyard alongside the Stephens family vault containing the family's remains which were initially interred in the chapel churchyard.

The ceremony in 1928 to open the new road to Minsterworth's Methodist Chapel, with Mrs Vyner Ellis in her car inaugurating the route. Until recently, an old wooden sign was attached to the entrance gate to the chapel road reading 'Entrance to Minsterworth Methodist Church'.

Sadly, by the 1940's, the number of worshippers was beginning to dwindle. The chapel continued for a time but, by about 1970, the point was reached when the chapel could no longer continue. In addition, about this time the chapel building began to show the effects of subsidence. It finally closed in the early 70's and by 1978 only the shell of the building remained. The Methodist Society then sold the land on which it stood, including also Old Chapel House, to local builder Mr Tony Laken. It was he who in the end undertook the demolition of the chapel and the rebuilding of the old house on The Street now known as 'Chapel Cottage'.

Exterior and interior scenes of the Minsterworth Methodist Chapel during the demolition in 1978. Inset: The roundel plaque from the front of the chapel; this was rescued and still exists but no longer in a recognisable state.

This is almost the end of the story of the chapel. It of course still remains a fond memory for some older residents of Minsterworth, but to all intents and purposes it is now something of the past. There are however still two tangible objects from the chapel to remind us of its one-time presence in Minsterworth. Ironically, one relates to the very end and the other to the very beginning of the chapel's existence. When the chapel was decommissioned, a decision had to be made as to the Stephens' family vault in the small graveyard there. Commemorated on the stone covering the vault were Richard Stephens himself (d.1897), his wife Martha (d.1903) and seven of their offspring, spanning the years 1846 to 1884. Sadly, two of their children died as babies and none of the others (4 boys and a girl) lived beyond the age of 31. It was decided that the family's remains and the stone covering the vault should be transferred to the churchyard at St Peter's parish church. The reburial duly took place on 21st June 1974 under Home Office supervision and the original single gravestone can still be seen close to the church on the south side.

The Stephens family double-facetted gravestone in St Peter's churchyard showing the face carrying details of William and Martha Stephens. Details of seven of their children are engraved on the other side.

And so to the other object, namely a clay pipe. Some while back, the author was presented with an old clay pipe by Mr Dennis Coldwell who, with his wife Barbara, had bought the new house built on the site of the old chapel. When they first arrived, the lowest wall footings of the chapel were still in place and it was as these were being removed that the clay pipe was found buried in the rubble core of the old wall. Still in a good and clean condition and with a corn ear decoration on the bowl, its shape fits the style of pipes being made locally around the 1840/1850s, i.e. about the time the chapel was built. It must have been put down by one of the

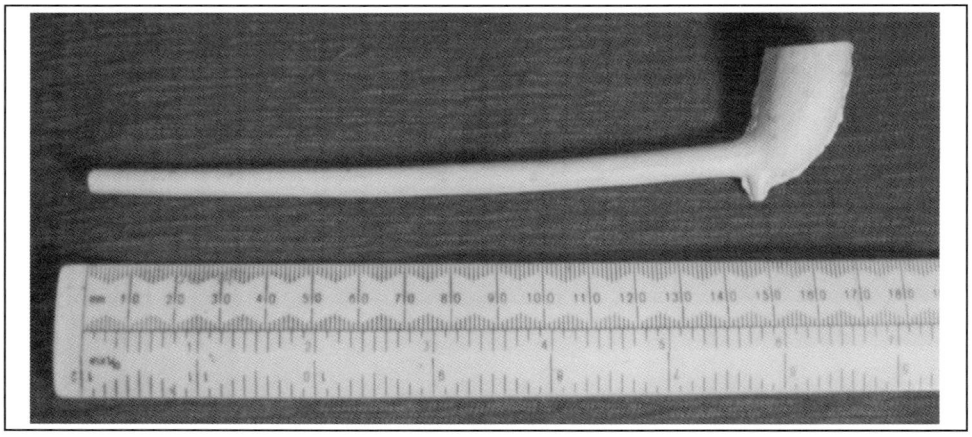

Clay pipe found in the wall of Minsterworth Methodist Chapel.

chapel's builders over 150 years ago and forgotten. It almost seems to have emerged to ensure that we don't forget those early Methodist pioneers of Minsterworth and their now long-gone chapel at Calcotts Green.

VII.

GOING, GOING, GONE

The ancient Greek proverb has it that "Change is the only Constant". This applies everywhere and certainly to Minsterworth where, over the centuries, so much has changed. Sometimes this is evident from historical records about something long-vanished, sometimes it resides within living memories of older folk and in some cases it is happening even before our very eyes. For Minsterworth, It is worth examining this topic from the aspects of our ever-present River Severn, from the roads and tracks by which centuries of "Minsterworthies" have moved about, to the buildings and other structures that have been lost or changed.

The River Severn

Given Minsterworth's close association with the river over the ages, it must be right to start here. Once described as 'Gloucestershire's gateway to the outside world', the River Severn was of considerable importance to this part of the country and certainly in the development of Minsterworth. In medieval times it was used to carry military supplies up to Gloucester and for centuries it was a principal route for all kinds of river vessels carrying cargoes of grain, fruit and other food produce, stone for road building, coal and timber. Many of these vessels put in at the Church Landing Yard or at Duni for loading or unloading and repairs, and numerous riverside houses doubled up as hostelries providing much needed comforts for the sailors whilst their vessels were moored up awaiting the next tide. In the early 17th century almost a quarter of Minsterworth's adult male population were sailors and up to five shipwrights worked here. With its tides, tricky currents and hazardous channels, the river was always difficult for navigation and it was this that finally led to the opening in 1827 of the Gloucester-Sharpness Canal. This reduced the journey by a half and drastically curtailed the use of the river as a waterway. Some reflection of how things were (and continued for a time after this) is provided by Brian Waters in his book "Severn Tide" published in 1947:

> Minsterworth is a curiously independent village with a taste for trade with foreign parts. A sixty-year-old man repairing the river bank told me how puzzled he had been as a child at hearing his grandmother ask a passing bargee to bring her back a 'nest of pans' from Bridgewater, since these utensils could be bought cheaper there than in Gloucester. Fruit was exported to Newport in Sam Wathan's sloop, and Minsterworth was mightily proud of the fact that its merchant navy was able to dock in Newport harbour free of dues, for the village being in the Duchy of Lancaster is absolved from paying dues and tolls in harbours and markets.

Boat building also continued even into the 20th century. Up to at least the 1930s, local carpenter and blacksmith Bert Prosser counted boat building among the services he provided, and a traditional Minsterworth salmon punt built at Prosser's yard in 1910 is now in a national maritime museum.

And then there was fishing, which for centuries was also of considerable economic importance for Minsterworth and a major source of employment and livelihood for village folk. Lamprey, salmon, eels and elvers were the most prized catches. Fish have always been caught on the river by means of nets and baskets and, in the case of eels, by means of the traditional Minsterworth eel spear. Throughout the medieval period however the principal means of catching fish was the fish weir, a 'V'-shaped fence-like structure of timber and brushwood built out into the river for distances of many metres with a large basket trap at the apex of the 'V' forming a trap for fish coming downstream on the receding tide

Artist's impression of a medieval fishweir (not to be confused with the putcher weirs used in more recent times, mostly further downstream on the Severn). (M. Aston)

For centuries Minsterworth had up to three structures like this operating on the local stretch of river, as either royal, ecclesiastical or manorial possessions. One we are pretty certain was down at the Denny and two others operated in the vicinity of Minsterworth itself. Inevitably, especially given the narrowness of the river, a conflict of interests between shipping and fishing was bound to happen. This led to repeated attempts by the authorities, usually with limited effect, to regulate the scope of fish weir operations and the obstructions to navigation they caused. Finally, in 1531 during the reign of Henry VIII, an Act of Parliament was made, a part of which read:

> …. Considering the great damage and losses which have happened … by and through mills, mill dams, wears (i.e. weirs) etc in and upon some rivers….to the inestimable damages of the Commonwealth and Realm … and despite diverse and many provisions having been made and ordained, none are sufficient remedy for the reformation of the premises

The Act then directed the king's "Commissioners of Sewers" to:

> ….. survey the said impediments and cause to be made corrected, repaired, amended, put down or reformed as the case may require.

On the Severn the effects of this regulation do not really appear until 4 years later in 1535 when the many fish weirs on the river were finally destroyed on the king's orders. Of course, fishing in other forms continued to be a major activity on the Severn for centuries afterwards. Long net fishing for salmon and the catching of eels and elvers were thriving commercial concerns in Minsterworth right into the 20th century but had almost ceased by the 1970s.

No bridges spanning the river have been known in Minsterworth but the river was regularly crossed either by ferry or by foot. A medieval fieldname of 'Stanilade' (i.e. stoney lode or ferry) located probably in Cornham is believed to indicate an ancient ford across the river there and people still talk of persons crossing the river on foot at the Denny Rock when water levels were sufficiently low. The ferry boat service between Minsterworth and the old Salmon Inn in Elmore Back is still remembered by older villagers. The importance of the ferry may be better understood when one realises that for centuries much of Elmore Back was part of Minsterworth manor and parish. The punt-like boat could take up to 8 or 10 people and passengers also included young children crossing to attend school in Minsterworth. Animals may also have been transported across by ferry: there is a suggestion that in the past cattle may have been able to cross at low tide.

Minsterworth poet F W Harvey (1888-1957) visualised a slightly different kind of scenario when he wrote (with tongue in cheek) his poem about Old William Fry of Minsterworth who decided to buy a pig from Elmore Back and got it back across the river in the ferry by making it drunk on perry! The last verse of the poem reads:

> He poured a goodish swig and soon
> As lazy as a day o' June -
> Piggy lay boozed, and so did bide
> Snoring, while him and Fry were taken
> 'Cross Severn and a' didn't waken
> Until the boat lay safely tied
> Up to a tree on t'other side

The ferry was operating at least until the early part of the 19th century and seems to have continued officially or unofficially up until shortly after World War II. Except for the survival of landing steps near to Pershbrook Cottage however, the ferry is no more.

Observing the tranquil scene along the banks of the river here , it is really hard to visualise the bustling, industrious and congested waterway it must once have been.

Roads and tracks

Today, as we make our way around the roads and lanes of Minsterworth, complaining either about the traffic congestion or the bad state of the road surfaces, how easy it is to think that it has always been this way, and to forget how people once moved around and through our village. When he was interviewed by BBC Radio Gloucestershire in 1996, then 93 years old Bert Prosser of Minsterworth claimed that the greatest contribution to change in the village was the road which in his time had transformed the sleepy village into a race track. He recalled that:

> When I was young there was no motor car, all there was were horses and traps. We used to play tops and marbles on the road, you know, out on the road, play tops and have a marble patch, all we had to do was get out of the way when a horse and trap came, that's all. The road was just a narrow country lane, had no kerbs nor ditches at the sides. It was made up of stone and mud rolled in with a steam roller…... Then "improvements" came: the road was widened and straightened. They cut off two bends near the Appletree and cut down lots of trees. The traffic has got worse and worse.

In theory the main road has been in the process of improvement since as far back as 1726 when the route was chosen to be the turnpike road from Gloucester to Chepstow. The Romans had shown us how to build metalled roads but after their withdrawal from Britain in the 5th century, and virtually right up to post medieval times, the roads of this country were mostly poorly surfaced, or not surfaced at all, what surface existed was constantly being crushed and ground down by horses hooves and wagon wheels so that in winter it was awash with mud and water and in summer rutted and dusty.

Writing in 1767, the English traveller and agriculturalist Arthur Young described the turnpike road from Gloucester to Newnham thus:

> I was infinitely surprised to find the same stony, hard, rough, and cursed roads, miscalled turnpikes, all the way from Gloucester to Newnham, which is 12 miles: it is all a narrow lane, and most infamously stony; it is the same stone as the other side of the Severn, but much harder, and consequently more jolting, and cutting to horses feet; nor is it so much as level, but rutts all the way; and what is remarkable, I found by them, that they build their wagons with their wheels full three inches nearer to each other than in eastern counties, which is surprising: a Norfolk or Suffolk wagon could not stir even this turnpike road.

Roads are after all not permanent features on the landscape and if we are to understand how things have changed, we have to look at the total picture of local roads, tracks and paths over a long period. Inevitably, the resultant picture is an overlay of features of different dates: of ancient roads and tracks of medieval or possibly even earlier date (many now largely obliterated). Later medieval or early post-medieval routes developed around emerging village settlements and still later, after a considerable time, the enclosure roads and turnpikes in the 18th and 19th centuries brought about profound changes to local road systems, forming the backbone of the modern road network we see about us today. The A48 for example started out as little better than a field track zigzagging its way across the parish and the old "main road" up to then had followed a totally different course.

Let's just look at the past evolution of two "roads" in Minsterworth.

The Old Road from Gloucester.
The route of this road left the main road west out of Gloucester at Over, crossed the fields in a more or less direct line through Lower Linton and entered the parish near Upper Moorcroft, proceeding on through Ham Green to Highcross. This section of the road has now been obliterated, thanks to centuries of farming activity and finally the construction in the 19th century of the railway to South Wales.

Very probably though this route into Gloucester, avoiding the A40 (Roman) road, was in the mind of the young Will Harvey when he wrote the words:

> I will not take the great road that goes so proud and high,
> Like the march of Roman legions that made it long ago;
> But I will choose another way, a little road I know ....
> (from Gloucestershire Friends, 1917)

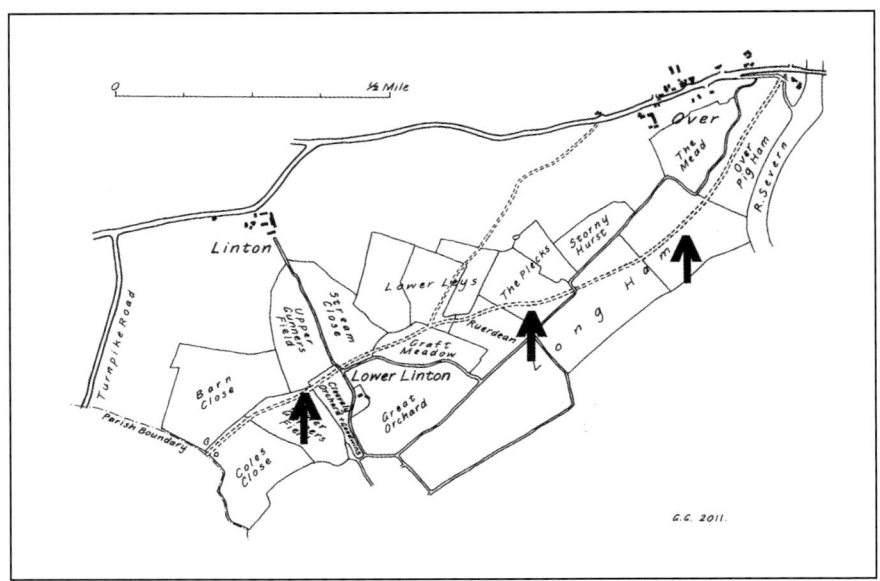

Abridged copy of an early 19th century tithe map for Churcham parish showing Over and Lower Linton and the line (arrowed) of the old road running up to the Minsterworth boundary. (With acknowledgement to Geoffrey Gwatkin who produced the original map)

Interestingly, on the 1757 map of Minsterworth, the newly turnpiked road to Gloucester appears not to cross the parish boundary towards Highnam but is shown turning sharply southwards to run alongside the parish boundary to the point where the old road leaves the parish as the way "to Gloucester". The continuation of the road through Minsterworth is only faintly traceable from features such as field boundaries and unconfirmed "traces of paving" shown on early Ordnance Survey maps. It is notable though that close examination of Upper Moorcroft Farm building shows that the western front of the building facing the A48 is of probably 18th century brick, whereas the opposite (probably 16th century) elevation of the house has close studded timberwork consistent with this being the 'posher' side of the

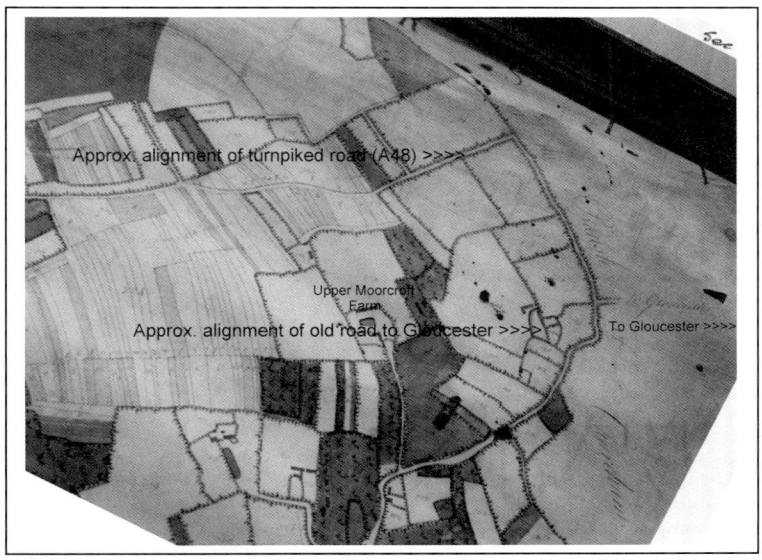

Detail from the 1757 map of the NE corner of Minsterworth parish with author's notes superimposed.

house intended to make an impression on travellers passing along the old road in earlier times. In the mid 1500s this section of the road appears to have been called Morcottes Lane. Upon reaching Highcross, the road becomes obvious following the modern alignment through Calcotts Green and along The Street and on to the west. In the mid 1500s The Street was called "Ham Street" and later "the highway from the church to the ham" and a road map from the late 1600s shows it as "the way to Newnham". A raised cobbled causeway that runs alongside The Street between Street End Cottage and the church is believed to have been constructed in the early post- medieval period or later for use during times of flood.

Incidentally, the position of Highcross in older times would have made it a significant crossroads location with the old road from Gloucester branching off to a secondary route (Watery Lane) leading to the Appletree and on to Highgrove; another (Pound Lane); and finally another leading into Cornham. It would be of no surprise to me if the local gallows were not standing at this point too—but maybe that's another story!

The Way to Churcham
We accept unquestioningly today that getting from Minsterworth to Churcham involves taking the A40 either via Highnam or Oakle Street but, given the

close associations between the two communities over the centuries, it can't always have been this way. In fact the hardier walkers of Minsterworth still go on foot to Churcham by way of a footpath that leaves the A48 roughly opposite the Old Vicarage and, like so many old public footpaths, it must once have been of much greater importance. From the A48, it proceeds across the fields to the Longbrook which it crosses at a place for centuries called Shadbridge and then climbs gradually up to Churcham church crossing the modern railway on the way. It seems likely that Churcham Lane leading to the A40 is a continuation of it.

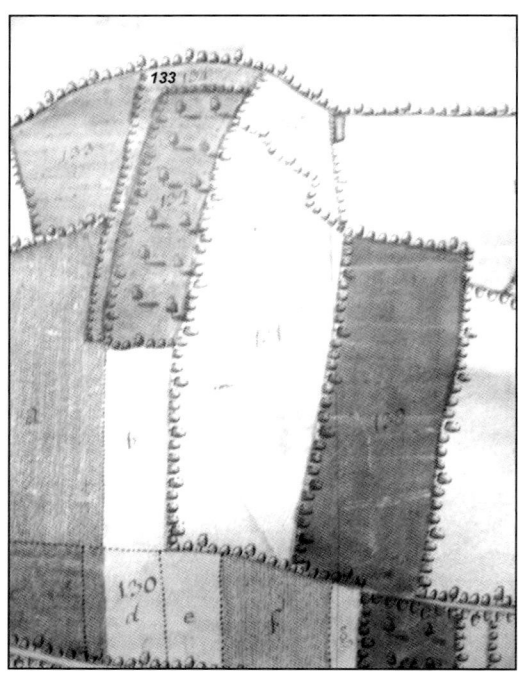

Detail from the 1757 map of Minsterworth showing part of the old route to Churcham. What is now the A48 is just visible at the bottom left corner of the picture and a section of the greenway heading north to the Longbrook shown by the long narrow strip of land (parcel no.133, called Shadbridge Meadow). The width of the strip indicates that this would once have been a relatively wide road or trackway capable of accommodating wide farm wagons and carts.

At the Minsterworth end, it would almost certainly have continued down towards the church and the old manorial centre (believed to have been where Tithe Cottage now stands) either via Bury Lane ("bury" being the term often referring to an ancient manorial centre) or via the track or bridleway leading down beside Pump Court. Although seemingly quite a narrow way, the latter has at some time obviously been quite wide enough for heavier traffic.

Buildings

No account of what has been in Minsterworth would be complete without looking briefly at its buildings and other structures. The 1757 estate map shows numerous now-disappeared structures scattered around the village, mainly around Hampton and the area of the lower road but, in most cases we are left to speculate what kind of buildings they were or what their purposes might have been. No doubt many of them would have been homes for the agricultural workers who were once the major workforce here.

We of course know of the many buildings which are within the living memory of older residents: places like the Methodist Chapel at Calcotts Green, the post office and telephone exchange originally at Pershbrook Cottage before moving for a time in 1924 to Graingers in Duni; also its neighbour Ferry Cottage (latterly the home of the Stephens family) which was demolished after being condemned and has been replaced by a telephone sub-station. Also in Duni was Bodnams Cottage which, until road widening in the 1960s, stood on the north side of the main road just east of the Oakle Street junction.

Bodnam's Cottage Minsterworth. In common with a number of older river-side houses, a large part of Bodnam's was constructed of slag blocks brought up-river mostly from copper works in Bristol.

Also worth mentioning is the old Pound, once essential for impounding stray farm animals. Minsterworth's pound stood inside the top corner of the field running up the west side of Pound Lane opposite old Pound Cottage. Some still remember seeing the stone-built remnants of the enclosure here. Today the spot is thickly overgrown but some remains of the structure may still be there.

We have no image of the old animal pound in Minsterworth but it quite probably resembled the pound in nearby Newnham which is shown here in its restored form.

Other just in-living-memory sites include the bakery near the church, the village's blacksmith forges (including one next to Rosedale on the Main Road which closed in the 1920s, as well of course as Bert Prosser's forge at Duni), Fanny Phelps' sweet and tobacco shop at the rear of Lyn Paddock, and the Farm Café demolished in 1997 to make way for Home Orchard bungalow. Add to these, other facilities like the former police station at Greenacres, the swimming pools at the Appletree, more garages along the Main Road and, of course, all those beautiful orchards that once graced the countryside, and it becomes easier to envisage Minsterworth as it was not so very long ago.

There are in addition truly ancient sites that have really long gone. Consider mills, which in early times were essential to the economy of any medieval manor either for grinding corn or raising water. Historic documents tell us that in the 1300s a mill at Duni was a Forest of Dean boundary mark, and just slightly earlier there is a reference to a "bridge of the mill", presumably Denny Bridge. This probable water-mill though may not have been in Minsterworth itself for at the time the miller was required to pay the lord of Minsterworth for the water he used. There is no reference in medieval documents to Minsterworth manor ever having a mill of its own. It is interesting therefore that among field names for Minsterworth in 1749 were two with the names "Windmill Acre" and "Windmill Piece". The 1839 tithe map for Minsterworth parish shows a group of small fields situated where Appithorne house is today called "Windmill Bush Piece" and "Windmill Hill". This place is one of the prominent high points in the village and a logical site for a windmill.

The earliest most common form of windmill was the post-mill, so-called because the body of the mill with its revolving sails was pivoted on a vertical wooden frame standing on a mound and it was turned to face the wind by means of a long pole extending out from the structure.

An old photograph of a typical post-mill standing on its mound (with acknowledgement to the NMR, www.pastscape.english-heritage.org.uk.). What is probably the remains of the mound for Minsterworth's windmill is still just visible beneath and beyond the road-side hedge immediately east of Appithorne.

We do not know when this mill was in operation but the 1757 map shows nothing at this place so maybe the mill was in existence for only a brief time prior to then and, by 1839, only the memory of it remained in the form of the "windmill" field names.

Most will be familiar with the parish's Old Vicarage built in the late 1800s. Few may know that it replaced an earlier vicarage house which stood on The Street immediately opposite the church . A vicarage of some sort or the other must have been on this site for a long time, certainly it seems since the 1600s, but we have only a sketchy idea of what it was like. We may assume that it was quite a modest structure - Minsterworth after all was not a particularly wealthy parish. We certainly know what the vicar of the day, the Rev. Arthur Nettleship, thought of it since, in an appeal to the Ecclesiastical Commissioners for financial help to build the new vicarage, he wrote:

> ….The present vicarage stands on so narrow a strip of ground there is not sufficient space for outbuildings and offices …. The vicarage which was formerly a carpenter's cottage is now but little better than one.

By dint of funds raised through grants and loans (not to mention the donation of the land for the new house by Mr William Syms of this parish), the Rev. Nettleship succeeded in raising £1350 to have his new, very splendid, vicarage built and the old house disappeared to became part of the vicarage garden. A modern house called Old Road House now occupies the site.

No less interesting perhaps are those buildings, once vibrant homesteads or work-related premises, that are literally disappearing before our eyes. Places on the main road like Ryders, Pound Cottage and, on the riverbank, Highlay and Poolend all of which are slowly disintegrating.

The Mitchell family at Pound Cottage around 1900. The cottage, now derelict, still stands at the top of Pound Lane.

Also of interest is a site just in from the river in the orchard between The Naight and Poolend. The map of 1757 shows a small square enclosure of land at this spot and, by 1839, the same plot is described as also having "a cottage and garden". According to the Ordnance Survey, the same premises is there in the late 1800s. No further formal record of this place or who occupied it has so far been found but we know that something there (albeit a ruin) existed well into the 20th century because John Browning, whose family lived at Poolend, remembers playing around it as a boy. Mr Eric Watkins of Elm Farm, who farms that land, also remembers having to skirt the ruins there when ploughing and of having to fill in a well there. Time and nature have taken over and today the only sign of anything ever having stood there is a low mound covered with nettles.

Going, going, gone indeed……..

VIII.
LITERARY LINKS

Think of Canterbury and Chaucer, Stratford-on-Avon and Shakespeare, Bath and Jane Austen, Slad and Laurie Lee, Oxford and Colin Dexter, Minsterworth and ……….? You may well feel that there are exceedingly few obvious literary associations for this small Severn-side village, but you would be wrong. In fact, history records quite a number of writers of various sorts associated in diverse ways with Minsterworth: from a medieval 'chronicler' to a 20th century Forest poet, picking up on the way an Elizabethan authority on heraldry, an Edwardian author of 'who dunnits' and others

Walter Map (c.1130-c.1209/10)

Walter Map was born of a Herefordshire border family, which seemingly was prosperous enough to have access to the English royal court of Henry II. He may have had his early schooling at Gloucester Abbey and then studies in Paris. Thereafter he appears to have risen in service both in the church and to the crown. He enjoyed the patronage first of the bishop of Hereford and later the bishops of Leicester and London. By 1173, he is also recorded as being in royal service, acting for a time as a royal itinerant justice. Such a situation inevitably brought wealth and status. He acquired numerous church livings and other properties around the country. One of the church benefices he possessed was the parish of Westbury-on-Severn (then under the diocese of Hereford) and, according to the list of past incumbents at Newnham parish church, he was also incumbent there in 1170.

But it is as a court chronicler that Walter Map is most notable, largely on the strength of a single written work entitled 'De Nugis Curialium' (lit. 'Of Courtly Trifles'). This drew on his experience at the royal court for much of its material. It consists of legends, tales and gossip about affairs at court and, as such, was intended more to entertain rather than inform. It has been suggested though that, with his *de Nugis* and through his collaboration with Geoffrey of Monmouth, Map had a hand in shaping the Arthurian legends. But Map's writings are generally perceived to be weak on actual historic facts and, for this reason, the work is not regarded by modern-day experts as being a reliable source for historical research.

But to get to the connection with Minsterworth. One chapter of the *De Nugis* deals retrospectively with the conflict between the Danish king Cnut and the Anglo-Saxon king Edmund Ironside early in the 11th century. Some of the action took place in Gloucestershire and is surrounded by intrigue, including treachery by one of Edmund's own servants. This is how Map tells it:

> Now this was the manner of it. Cnut had London and the parts beyond Icknield, Edmund the rest, and thus he happened to come to that coveted Minsterworth, the chapel of which I, thank God, today hold in right of its mother church of Westbury. But this servant when he saw it, with all the resources and amenities that belonged to it, flamed out into madness, and, minister of the devil as he was, put into the hole of his master's privy a large, sharp iron spit, and, preceding him as he came with a strong light of candles, suddenly turned them in another direction, that his master might fall into the snare unawares. He fell into it, and was pierced with a mortal wound, and had himself carried thence, and died at Ross, a royal town which with its church he gave to the church of Hereford which still owns it.

We need not dwell on Edmund's undignified end not least because there is great uncertainty about how he actually did die. Some sources suggest he died in Oxford, others in London and there is a legend that he was buried in the abbey at Glastonbury. Most authorities though agree that his death in November 1016 was 'in suspicious circumstances', probably engineered by King Cnut and his agents.

A 13th century depiction of Edmund Ironside and Cnut of the Danes in combat at the battle of *Assandun* (Ashingdon in Essex) in October 1016, when Cnut was victorious. (Google Images)

More significant for us perhaps is that Map felt he could write about 'all the resources and amenities' belonging to the 'coveted Minsterworth'. Given

Minsterworth's proximity to the royal centre of Gloucester and to the royal hunting lands of the Forest of Dean, it would not be surprising if at least a hunting lodge existed in Minsterworth and that Edmund may well have visited it when in the area. Also, to those who dismiss Map's story outright, it has been argued that such people underestimate the value of local tradition. As the vicar of Westbury and Minsterworth, Map would have been exposed to local historical tradition from Edmund's time. Also, since nobody ever regarded Edmund Ironside as a saint, the parson and people of Minsterworth could have had no motive for inventing fiction about his death. Their accounts are therefore no less preferable than those of other chroniclers of the time.

John Gwillim ((1550)-1621)

Sir John Gwillim of Minsterworth was among that exclusive group of royal officials known as 'heralds'.* The Gwillims, a family of Welsh descent, were prominent in the Gloucestershire-Herefordshire area.. Sir John's father, John Gwillim senior, was also known as John ap Gwillim of Westbury-on-Severn but it is clear that the family were also associated with Minsterworth. His son by the same name is best known as the author and publisher of a major work on English heraldry which remained the standard reference book on the subject for well over a hundred years and which even today is regularly used by working heralds.

We cannot be certain as to the extent the Gwillims regarded Minsterworth as their home but we know that in 1552 John Gwillim senior witnessed the will of a William Kynge of Moorcote, implying that he was well known in the parish. Upon his death in 1587, he was described as ' The Worshipful John Gwillim, lord of the Manor of Hatheways in the Parish of Minsterworth' (Hatheways was the name given to a sub-manorial estate of Minsterworth comprising lands around the centre of the village (roughly around today's Court), in Duni and in Westbury parish). John senior died at his manor court house in 1581 and apparently was given a heraldic burial by his son. Towards the end of the 16th century, the family were noted as leasing out and selling their properties in Minsterworth, suggesting that they were not by then fully resident in the parish.

---

* In medieval times heralds, distinguished by the colourful tabards they wore, were employed as diplomatic messengers either moving between courts or, at time of war, between opponents on the battle field. In peacetime, they also took part in the running and ceremony of the tournament where they used their expertise at identifying knights from their armorial displays. Over time, and as the possession of armorial symbols became popular among the new gentry families, the heralds were charged under the Royal College of Arms with the care of genealogies and the allocation of armorial shields.

Sir John, was born in Hereford we think in 1550, the elder of two sons. He studied at the Cathedral school there and then at Brasenose College Oxford. By 1575 he was married to Frances (from the Dennys family of Siston in Gloucestershire) and their first child (another John Gwillim) was born in 1578. How and when John came to be involved in heraldry is not known but by 1595, at the age of 45, he had begun writing his 'Display of Heraldrie'. This colourful opus, containing over 280 pages and 500 woodcuts of armorial shields, was eventually published in 1610. It contained the details of the arms of many noble English families and represented the first authoritative methodical exposition of English armorial symbols. Before this, in 1604, an Earl Marshal's warrant was issued permitting him to wear the tabard of Portsmouth 'pursuivant extraordinaire' and in 1613 he was created 'rouge croix pursuivant' to the Crown for which he received a salary from the College of Arms.

A contemporary description of the second edition of the work (in 1632) read thus:

> A Display of Heraldrie: Manifesting a More Easie Access to the Knowledge Thereof Than Hath Beene Hitherto Published By Any, Through The Benefit Of Method, Wherin It Is Now Reduced By The Study and Industry Of John Guillim, Late Pursuivant At Armes

The frontspiece of John Gwillim's ' A Display of Heraldrie' first published in 1610

John Gwillim died in 1621, supposedly in Minsterworth, and is thought to have been buried in London. Although not a name on everyone's lips today, in his time he achieved fame for his scholarship on the subject of heraldry. He was also known to many other prominent Elizabethans including the notable English historian and cartographer John Speed (1551/2-1629), who described him as 'his worthy and well-deserving friend'.

Arthur Conan Doyle (1859-1930)

This is a true-life fairy tale romance involving a modest farmer's daughter from Minsterworth and a national literary giant knighted for his service to literature. The lady in question was Louisa, the younger daughter of Jeremiah Hawkins of Lower Moorcroft Farm Minsterworth and the knight was Sir Arthur Ignatius Conan Doyle, the creator of the Sherlock Holmes novels. Through her marriage to Conan Doyle, Louise (or 'Touie', as she was known in the Hawkins family) became Lady Conan Doyle. The couple had children of their own and the tale could have had a classic happy ending, but sadly Louisa became ill and died still quite young.

During the 1700s and 1800s, a Hawkins family of Minsterworth held substantial amounts of land and property including the freehold of Lower Moorcroft Farm in Minsterworth. One member of the family was a Jeremiah Hawkins (b.1795) who, along with his wife Emily, had moved about quite a bit, first to Monmouth and then in the 1860s to Leckhampton near Cheltenham. By the time of the 1871 census however, old Jeremiah was back at Lower Moorcroft Farm where he was cared for by his two unmarried daughters until his death. It was in 1884 that Louisa's young brother Jack became ill with the onset of cerebral meningitis and she and her mother together took him to Southsea in the hope of finding a cure. While there, Jack was seen by a local doctor, Conan Doyle, who took him in as a resident patient. Jack died in the following year but not before Conan Doyle and Louisa had become attracted to each other. They were married that same year, 1885, in Thornton-in-Lonsdale, Lancashire where Doyle's mother lived.

Young Conan Doyle grew up in Edinburgh in not particularly affluent circumstances. Fortunately he benefitted from support from wealthy relatives enabling him to attend Edinburgh University Medical School. He graduated from there in 1881, eventually settling in Portsmouth where he built up a successful doctor's practice. He had started writing as a student but this side of his work developed significantly during the 1880s and 1890s. It was in 1886, one year into his marriage to Louisa, that he shot to fame with 'Study In Scarlet', the novel that first introduced Sherlock Holmes and Dr Watson together. Although outwardly a bluff and genial character, Conan Doyle was an intensely intellectual man with strong tendencies towards the occult. By contrast, Louisa was neither gifted nor well-read One source describes her as:

> A simple loving soul who would keep house for him, bear his children, and even augment his funds with a small private income of her own. .... Victorian women were not supposed to be trailblazers. Society had marked them out as homemakers, housekeepers, mothers and nurses. ... exuding femininity and warmth. 'Touie' fitted the bill perfectly. (.Richard Lancelyn Green; *Louise Hawkins and her Family.)*

Though not beautiful in the classic sense, Louisa had a round face, wide mouth, brown hair, widespread blue eyes and a placid nature all of which must have appealed to Conan Doyle. In 1889, by which time the Conan Doyles were living in London, a daughter, Mary, was born and three years later a son, Alleyne. Around this time it was becoming clear though that Louisa's health was failing and Conan Doyle took her abroad more than once to help cure her. Her illness was eventually diagnosed as tuberculosis and the family moved to South Norwood for its healthier air.

Young Louisa Hawkins of Minsterworth, destined to become Lady Conan Doyle (1857-1906).

Thanks to the devoted care she received, Louisa lingered on but, on 4th July 1906, she died tragically in her husband's arms and was buried in Hindhead Surrey.

Conan Doyle and Louisa try out a new tricycle outside their house in South Norwood.

Conan Doyle's reputation as a writer was now at its zenith, and in 1906 (the same year of Louisa's death) he was knighted for services to literature. In 1907, he married again, this time to a Jean Blyth Leckie whom he had known and been discreetly seeing for ten years or more (but that's another story ….). He continued writing into the late 1920s until his death in 1930.

As for his and Louisa's daughter Mary, by now she was fully independent on the strength of her Hawkins inheritances. Her possessions included properties in and around Minsterworth such as Highlay, Chapel Cottage and Weir House, in due course Lower Moorcroft Farm also fell into her hands. She had been working at her father's Psychic Bookshop near Westminster Abbey, but after his death she moved to Richmond and then Twickenham, where she died in 1976, aged 87.

F W (Will) Harvey (1888-1957)

For many local people, Will Harvey's links with Minsterworth are only too well known. Also, much has been written about this Gloucestershire poet, his life and work, most notably in an admirable biography of 'F W Harvey: Soldier, Poet' written by Anthony Boden. Harvey wrote powerful poetry not only about his war experiences but also about his love for the Gloucestershire countryside. At times moving, often humorous and sometimes in the local dialect, his verses are an expression of his profound love of the natural world around him and of the West Gloucestershire folk he knew so well. Harvey, like his close friends Ivor Gurney and Herbert Howells, was one of a highly talented generation of poets and musicians to emerge from Severn-side at this period.

Frederick William Harvey was born in 1888 at Murrell's End in Hartpury parish, the first-born of Howard and Matilda ('Tillie') Harvey. Howard Harvey was a farmer and a successful dealer in heavy horses, which he sold to local farmers and to breweries to pull their drays. When Will was three years old, the family moved to Minsterworth and set up home at the Redlands, a fine late Georgian farmhouse across the road from today's Appletree Inn. Over the next six years, three more sons were added to the family (Eric, Roy and Bernard) and a daughter (Gladys). The Redlands was a happy family home and it was while there that Will grew to love the surrounding water meadows , the orchards and, of course, the River Severn. He and his friends Gurney and Howells would walk together for miles talking and singing and enjoying the countryside round about.

Will attended King's School in Gloucester and, when fourteen, was sent for a time to a boarding school in Lancashire. The Harvey boys were all keen sportsmen, playing both football and cricket. In 1910, Will himself was a founder member and captain of the Minsterworth football team and, of this time, Will's son Patrick, in a letter to the author, writes that:

> Will and his brothers, and possibly a Prosser or two, founded the football team in Minsterworth and they had a reputation for rough play typical of the All Blacks!

By this time, the family had decided that Will should study to be a solicitor and he was articled to the Gloucester legal firm of Frank Treasure in St John's Lane.

A Harvey family snapshot, taken outside the Redlands in 1910. Will is sitting front right and his mother Matilda (or 'Tillie' as she was known in the family) is seated at the centre of the group.

After an unsuccessful attempt in 1911, Will passed his legal examinations in 1912, qualifying him to be a solicitor's assistant. It was around this time that he began to show himself to be a gifted poet, and in 1912 he wrote his well-known poem 'I Love Old Minsterworth', with the opening lines:

> I love old Minsterworth. I love the trees:
> And when I shut my eyes they are most clear,
> Those leafy homes of wren and red-breast dear,
> Those winter traceries so black and light. ....

Sadly, a war that was to bring momentous changes was just around the corner and, in 1914, Will along with his brother Eric joined the Gloucester Regiment. In March 1915, they were deployed to the front line in northern France where Will was promoted to lance-corporal. That same year, he took part in a night reconnaissance for which he gained a DCM and soon after he was commissioned. It was while on a lone reconnaissance mission the following year that Will was captured and for the next two years of the war he was captive in German prisoner-of-war camps. While at the front, Will continued writing, being a regular contributor to the 5th Glo'ster Gazette, and it was during his captivity that he wrote some of what is regarded as some of his most enduring verse.

F W Harvey, soldier, poet. Left, during World War I. Right, In 1920.

Apart from writing vividly, sometimes humorously, about the hardships and sufferings of war, Will also wrote nostalgically about home: such poems as 'On Dinny Hill the daffodil has crowned the year's returning....'*(Gloucestershire from Abroad)*, 'If we return, will England be just England still to you and me?' *(If We Return)* and 'I'm homesick for my hills again! To see above the Severn plain ..... The blue high blade of Cotswold lie' *(In Flanders)*. Many poems such as these that he managed to get back home were published in *A Gloucestershire Lad at Home and Abroad* (1916) and *Gloucestershire Friends* (1917). Perhaps his best known poem is 'From troubles of the world I return to ducks, beautiful comical things...' *(Ducks)*. Written in captivity, it was published along with more poems in 1919.

Physically and mentally exhausted Harvey returned home to Redlands in the Spring of 1919 to find himself at a crossroads in life. Writing was his passion but his marriage in 1921 to Anne, his Irish former nurse, made it sure that to make a living he had to return to working as a solicitor. His first position was in Swindon, where the Harveys lived in rented lodgings, and it was here that their first child, Eileen Anne, was born. Swindon was too dreary a place though and, as soon as he could, Will moved his family back to Minsterworth. After a brief sojourn at the Redlands, they moved to a rented cottage in Cranham. Yet another move followed to Broadoak, to a most unconventional dwelling made up of a pair of converted railway carriages, on the banks of the river Severn. There a second child, Patrick, was born.

A much later photograph of the Harvey family home at Broadoak taken just prior to its dismantling. The two arched doorways appear to mark the ends of the pair of railway carriages incorporated within the structure (Courtesy of Mrs Marion Jayne).

In 1925, Harvey set himself up as a solicitor in Lydney and the following year the family moved to a new home, High View, in Yorkley, which remained the family's final residence.

By conventional standards, Harvey was not especially successful as a solicitor, being more interested in less fortunate clients and poorer Forest folk whom, he felt, had been shabbily treated in some way. Over this time he continued to write, and more of his works were published. Now, though, still struggling with melancholy from his wartime experiences and increasingly disaffected - especially with the politics of the country - he finally resolved to make a professional career as a writer, and in 1930 sold off his Lydney practice. Thereafter, he became a familiar and popular figure around the towns and pubs of The Forest of Dean. He served in the Home Guard during the second World War and continued writing profusely and occasionally broadcasting on the radio. In 1947, an anthology of his works was published under the title 'Gloucestershire' containing much of the best of his writings and reflecting the many styles and moods that he had espoused over time. By the 1950s, Harvey's health was failing and, on 13th February 1957 he died at home in Yorkley. He was buried with others of the Harvey family in Minsterworth churchyard, close to the river and the orchards that he loved so much.

H G Wells (1866-1946)

Disbelief could well be the reaction to being told that there is a connection between the small village of Minsterworth and this world famous writer and founder of modern science fiction. It is true though. For much of the last half of the 19th century, Elm Farm in Minsterworth was occupied by a Mr Charles Wells. Charles' brother was Joseph Wells, the father of H G Wells, and it is recorded that Joseph on occasions stayed with his brother in Minsterworth (usually when he was between jobs) so knew the village well.

Herbert George (H.G.) Wells was born in Bromley (Kent) into a family of modest means. At the age of 14 he left school and took up employment for a time first in a draper's shop then in a chemists. Working life had no pleasure for him however and, although not a good student, in 1884 he became a trainee teacher, eventually entering the Normal School (now the Royal College) of Sciences in South Kensington on a government scholarship for trainee teachers. There he studied biology, zoology, physics and geology. By now H.G. had become a resentful and rebellious young man and, as his enthusiasm for study waned, so he began to take an interest in literature and socialist politics. It was during the summer of 1886 that Joseph Wells sent H.G. to stay for a month with his uncle Charles at Elm Farm, hoping that it would take his son away from the distractions of student life in London and cause him seriously to consider his future. H.G. appears to have found life in Minsterworth rather dull but not necessarily a waste of time; in his own autobiographical notes he writes:

> I had forgotten how very definite my literary ambitions had already become….My apprehensions though justifiable were not justified; I was given another chance and did not after all write to the scholastic agents. My father arranged for me to stay for a month with my Uncle Charles, a small farmer at Minsterworth near Gloucester. There, so soon as my anxiety about my return was dispelled, I set myself to write a paper on Socialism with which to open the autumn session of the Debating Society.

In fact, in 1887, H.G. left the Normal School without taking a degree, only to succumb to a period of ill health. It was during this time that he began to write copiously scientific articles and books. His first major novel, *The Time Machine*, was published in 1888 and this was followed by his famous *War of the Worlds* (1898) and a series of other novels unsurpassed for their imagination and visionary power. A slightly later book, *World Set Free'* (1914), even prophesised the atomic bomb.

Successive marriages and affairs were a mark of his life spent mostly in London but H G Wells was now world famous and a member of the country's literary elite. His work *The War of the Worlds* in particular became a world success and was adapted for numerous radio and screen presentations. The literary world has much to be thankful for that the young Wells resolved to make writing his life.

Postscript.

In the summer of 1950, the BBC Radio Light Programme ran a serialised adaptation of Wells' *War Of the Worlds*. The script of the novel was adapted for broadcasting by a certain Jon Manchip White, whose feature article on the work appeared in the BBC Radio Times issue for 28th May to 3rd June. Now read on…

Jon Manchip White (1924-   )

The name of Jon Manchip White is better known today in North America where, now an American citizen, he is a distinguished writer and academic. Before moving from the UK to the USA in the mid 1960s however, Manchip White had already earned academic honours and become a successful writer of novels, non-fiction and film and TV scripts. Less well-known is that Manchip White and his young family lived for a short time in Minsterworth Court and their two daughters attended Minsterworth school.

John Ewbank Manchip White was born in 1924 to an Anglo-Welsh family in Cardiff, his father being the managing director of a prominent South Wales shipping company. After a boarding school education in London, he was in 1941 awarded an exhibition scholarship in English at Cambridge. This was wartime however and, in 1943 - at the age of 19, he enrolled into the Royal Navy and for a time served at sea escorting convoys across the Atlantic. Towards the end of the war, he accepted an opportunity to join the Welsh Guards and served with them until the war's end on duties which included standing guard at Windsor Castle. It was on VE Day that he first met his future wife Valerie who had been a nurse during the war. Once able to do so and already writing novels and poems he returned to Cambridge where he extended his academic horizons to include prehistoric history and anthropology

In 1950 he graduated with honours in English, prehistoric archaeology and oriental languages (principally ancient Egyptian).

On the strength of his qualifications he was offered a post as keeper of Egyptian and Assyrian artefacts at the British Museum but to supplement his income he started writing scripts for BBC radio plays, eventually becoming a script editor for the newly-established BBC television service. For reasons not clear from the record, he left the museum in the early 1950s and took up a post in the Foreign Office where he worked for four years. In 1956, he decided to concentrate full-time on screen writing, which led to him travelling widely around Europe, writing for a number of epic films of the day and eventually becoming European story editor for Walt Disney.

The circumstances leading to the Manchip Whites coming to Minsterworth are far from clear, but local residents with memories going back to the 1960s recall their being in the village then and residing at Minsterworth Court. A search through electoral roll registers for Minsterworth for that time shows that Manchip White and his wife first appeared at The Court in 1960 where they stayed until at least 1964. Some as children also remember attending Minsterworth school with the two Manchip White girls (appropriately named, given the family's Welsh origins, Bronwen and Rhiannon). Perhaps it was that Minsterworth provided a quiet and stable home base away from the pressures of London, where creative writing could be done and the young family could thrive.

Minsterworth School recorder players at the Cheltenham Competitive Music Festival in 1962 or 1963. The group includes young Rhiannon Manchip-White (circled). (photograph provided by Mrs E Savage)

This situation was not to last long for, by the mid-1960s, for reasons not apparent in the record, Manchip White decided to change his circumstances once again and move with his family to North America. In 1967, he accepted a position in creative writing at the University of Texas in El Paso which led to a full professorship. Ten years later he became Professor of English at the University of Tenessee in Knoxville, at the same time becoming an American citizen.

Over the years, Manchip White has written or edited a vast number of books covering subjects as diverse as everyday life in Ancient Egypt, North American Indians and memories of a Welsh childhood.

Jon Manchip White, photographed in the USA.

He is also credited with having written for innumerable films and is identified in particular with several major apocalyptic shock-horror productions such as *The Day of the Triffids* (1962), *Crack in the World* (1965), *What to do when the Russians come* (1984) - not forgetting of course that radio adaptation of H G Wells' *War of the Worlds*.

Manchip White continues to live in North America and one American source in 2001 described him as:

> A balding man with a moustache, English reserve and speaking with
> a careful accent hardly diluted by half a lifetime in the USA..

Following his life story and diverse professional progress, one could be excused contemplating that Manchip White might easily have become a real-life Indiana Jones or even a British intelligence agent. Instead, he chose to become a full-time writer.

IX.

'A GOOD ALL ROUND MAN':
The Life and Work of Bert Prosser of Minsterworth.

Throughout time, in just about every village in the country there have been one or two individuals who stand out for the special contribution he or she has made to the local community. Regardless of the period and of their status in society, such people constitute a rich seam in the ore of life in that place and are remembered well beyond their lifetime. One such person is Bert Prosser (1903-1997) of The Forge, Minsterworth who spent virtually his whole lifetime living and working in the village and devoting his energies to the well being of the village and its inhabitants. According to local trade directories of the 1930s, he was described as a carpenter, builder, undertaker, boat builder, wheelwright, shoeing and general smith, repairer of all kinds of agricultural machinery. An exceptional range of specialist skills, but on top of this, he was also a mainstay in the affairs of the village generally - its church, parish council and village hall among others - and his knowledge of the history and topography of the parish was formidable.

In May 1997, not long before his death, Bert was interviewed by BBC Radio Gloucester's presenter Stephen Wright in one of his "Country Matters" programmes. The two chatted for the best part of an hour during which Bert, in his soft West Gloucestershire burr, spoke extensively of his life and work. At the end of it, Stephen Wright, felt moved to say:

> Every so often, one gets to meet people who know so much and are absolutely in tune with what is and was. We are all privileged to have people like Mr Prosser with such experience and knowledge.

This was a sentiment that those who knew Bert and whose lives had been touched by him would certainly agree with.

Albert George Prosser was born in 1903 in Stoneyard Cottages at the west end of Minsterworth, being the middle child of three (older sister Lucy and younger brother James (Jim). His father, also called George and also Minsterworth-born, served as gardener to the local gentry family of Viner-Ellis's. His grandfather William Prosser (d. 1906) who lived at nearby Bodnams Cottage had been coachman and gardener also for the Viner-Ellis's and all his earlier Prosser forebears were closely involved with the land and river in both Minsterworth and Elmore. Bert's pedigree also took in William (Bill) Prosser of The Pole Yard and Forge, Minsterworth, an uncle by marriage, who among other things built long-net salmon punts for use on the Severn (an example of his work from around 1910 is now in the collection of the National Maritime Museum).

When Bert was still a small boy, his family moved to Lymington (in Hampshire) to keep house for a branch of the Viner-Ellis family there. According to the national census, they were there in 1911 and, in later years, Bert spoke of seeing the Titanic sailing down the Solent (an event that happened in 1912). However, in 1914 when the recently widowed Mrs Viner-Ellis returned to Minsterworth with her children, the Prosser family moved back to the village with them. The Prossers took up residence in Duni Villa next to Bodnams, the old family home. From then on, Bert remained in, and closely attached, to Minsterworth for the rest of his life.

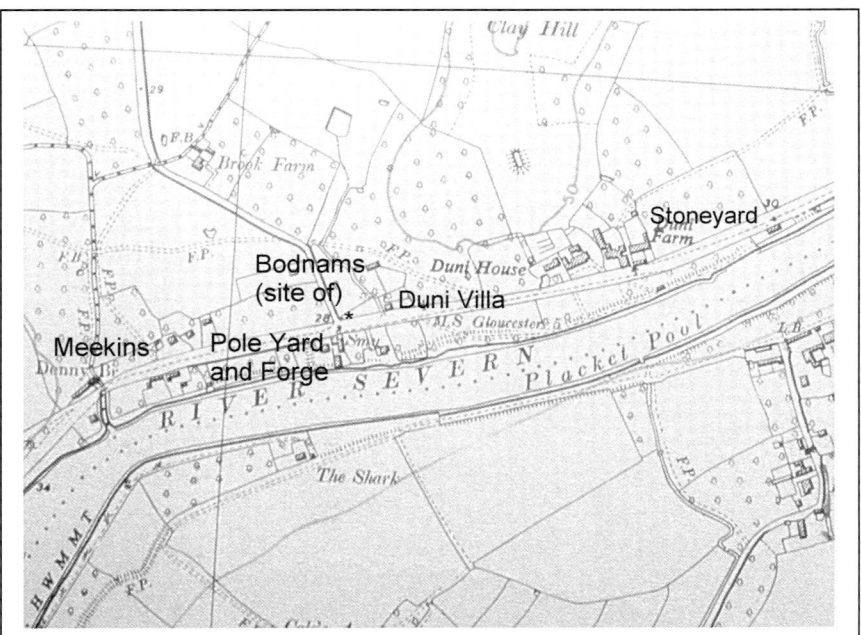

Various Prosser family homes in Minsterworth. Detail from a pre-1930 Ordnance Survey map of Minsterworth with the locations of The Pole Yard and Forge, Meekins, the original site of Bodnams Cottage, Duni Villa and Stoneyard Cottage added.

From early on, the Prosser family were worshippers at the parish church of St Peter's where Bert started singing in the church choir as a boy of 11 and later joined the bell ringing team. It is said in the family that he won a scholarship for a place at Gloucester's Crypt School, which may well be true but he does not appear to have taken up the place. His first venture into the workplace came when, as a teenager, he became appreciated with the then cart and wagon builders C Healey and Sons of Westgate Street Gloucester. How long he stayed with Healey's is not clear but by 1923 he had taken up a new apprenticeship with the wheelwright and carpenter Oliver Daniels in Moreton Valence, a commitment that involved him in a daily cycle ride to and from his work via Gloucester of around 15 miles each way (quite a bit less if he took his cycle across the river). This came to an end two years later in 1925 when Mr Daniels retired and Bert had to find new work. He could not though have received a better reference from Mr Daniels which, in retrospect, was very telling:

> During the time that Albert George Prosser has been employed by me, Fourteen months, I have always found Him to be a First Class Workman, in fact I couldn't wish for One better. He is Honest & straight, & an excellent timekeeper & I can fully recommend Him as a Wheelwright, Bodybuilder & Carpenter. (He is a good all round Man).

It is believed that at this point Bert attended the Gloucester College of Technology to study building but available records throw no further light on this. If true though, this training would have expanded his skills still further.

By this time, England was entering a period of economic recession when work was not always readily available. It was fortunate therefore that Bert was able to complete his training with his uncle William (Bill) Prosser at the Forge in Minsterworth. Subsequently, in 1933, Bill Prosser retired and Bert (then 30 years old) took over the business which was to occupy him for the rest of his working life. It was not all work though. He was a keen footballer, playing for Minsterworth AFC, and also a cricketer, playing for the highly-regarded Highnam Cricket Club and, very probably too, the Minsterworth parish church team (set up in 1909). We know from his own words that Bert also enjoyed catching elvers from the river along with most others of the local men.

Following the outbreak of World War II, one of the more significant happenings in Minsterworth was that Hygrove House in the village was acquired by the Zurich and General Accident and Liability Company as its wartime headquarters. The company's management had beforehand warned its staff that Minsterworth was "the country" and that they should make efforts to enjoy it (short of indulging in poaching). They did not however warn their young female staff of the charms of

Bert, wearing his goalkeeper outfit, pictured with the Minsterworth AFC team during the 1922-23 season.

Bert photographed with the rest of the Highnam Cricket Club team in 1928.

young Minsterworth men. One of their young ladies was Joan Francis (from Beckenham, Kent) who in course of time fell for Albert George. The two were married in 1945 in Minsterworth Church and together they moved into Meekins Cottage, just down the road from The Forge. During the war, Bert had served in the local Special Constabulary (finishing up as sergeant) and his own record book shows that within two weeks of war being declared he had voluntarily fitted black-out blinds to all the windows of the village hall. Already, his public spiritedness and involvement in village affairs were beginning to show. In 1947, Uncle Bill died and Bert and Joan (now known to everyone as "Jane") moved from Meekins into The Forge which became their permanent home. Not long after, a daughter Susan was added to the family.

The blacksmith was among the most important trades in any village. Horses needed shoeing regularly, tools of all sorts including domestic and farming implements had to be made or repaired, and wagons and other horse-drawn conveyances required regular attention especially repairs to wheels. Since earliest times there were blacksmiths in Minsterworth, as many as three or four at one time, but there are few records of where they were located. Throughout the 19th century though it is known that a forge existed on the site of Rosedale on the main road. In 1851, the blacksmith's shop there was apparently run by a lady who employed two journeymen.

We do not know how long a forge at Duni had existed but an estate map of 1757 shows structures on the site opposite Oakle Street and buildings are there on an 1839 map of Minsterworth along with a river-side plot to the immediate west described as "timber yard" (presumably the area later known as "Poleyard"). By the early 20th century, the site comprised a brick-built residence and, adjoining it on the east side, the forge building itself with direct access on to the main road. Additionally there were a carpenter's shop complete with circular and band saws, and a small paint store. A river landing yard facilitated the unloading of materials from the river and a slipway was there for boats. Also in the open yard on the ground was the heavy iron circular wheelwright's plate on which were assembled the component parts of the wheel, namely the hub (or 'nave'), spokes and felloes (pronounced 'fellies'- the sections making up the wooden rim), prior to the hot iron tyre being fitted and shrunk with cold water.

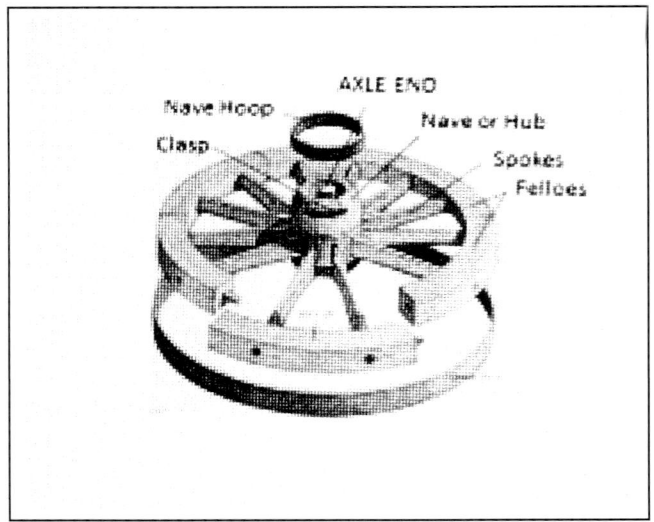

Component parts of the wheel as it would be fitted on to the wheelwright's plate.

With the advent of motor cars and tractors of course the demand for blacksmiths' services began to diminish and many of the skilled craftsmen were obliged to diversify into other trades such as, in Bert Prosser's case, building and carpentry.

When interviewed for the radio in later life, Bert recalled the various devices employed in his blacksmithing, including the sling used to lift the legs of a large cart horse off the ground so that it could not kick. Most of the forge's equipment has long been disposed of but the work that went on there remains in the memories of past associates in the village. His expertise as a blacksmith and wheelwright was also recorded for posterity by the Cotswold Countryside Museum formerly at Northleach, and the Gloucester City Folk Museum has in its collection a number of domestic items made at 'Mr. Prosser's forge in Minsterworth'.

His woodworking skills and the knowledge of boat building gained from his uncle made it inevitable that Bert would also manufacture boats in his river-side workshop. Demand may not have been great and there may not have been much money in it, but there is good evidence that a number of boats were made. A photograph from around 1936 shows a boat under construction in The Forge's carpentry shop and written records indicate that as late as 1993 Fred Rowbotham, the former District Engineer of the Severn River Board and noted expert on all Severn river matters, remembered Mr Prosser building several very good boats for him.

A clinker-built rowing boat under construction in Bert Prosser's carpentry shop sometime around 1936.

Coffin making and undertaking which Bert took up in the 1930s, also from his uncle, was a further logical extension to his woodworking. Originally every coffin was made entirely from scratch, including the making of 'kerf' cuts in the elm-planks necessary for curving and shaping the coffin sides. By the 1940s, so Bert has told us, he was able to buy-in pre-shaped boards from Bristol. Once assembled, the inside of the coffin had to be lined with hot pitch. In the radio interview Bert, in his whimsical way, spoke of his undertaking work thus:

> I suppose I was quite popular… I gave a 'good' funeral—you know people with money an' that. Another thing, I was fortunate in having four bearers all six feet high, all dressed in navy blue suits. You could never find four six-footers - it was a job to find'em. There was always a motor hearse. We could make the coffin, dress it, put it on a handcart and wheel him to a house at the top of the parish and we could do all that in one day.

In forty odd years of undertaking, he arranged around 300 funerals in and around Minsterworth, including that of the poet F W Harvey.

The woodworking also took in the making of ladders, in particular those traditionally designed for harvesting fruit in the orchards, with narrow tops and wider bottoms and iron spurs attached to the feet for penetrating the ground. As long as there were so many fruit orchards in the area, there was always a demand for Prosser's ladders like these. The Forge also had the distinction of possessing a relatively rare 40-rung ladder which was used for building work at height such as at the church. It was by no means an uncommon sight to see this enormous ladder being transported around the parish on a handcart or even sometimes carried balanced amazingly on the shoulder of one man, either Bert or one of his mates (his uncle Charlie and brother Jim were among those who worked with Bert).

From his earliest years in business however Bert was inclined towards building and it is in this capacity that he will be most remembered. In fact the business invoice he used in the 1940s, whilst listing all his skills, gave prominence to that of "builder". Whether it was a new construction or repairs to an existing structure, from repairing the church roof to building the all-important wells and septic tanks around the village, few of the older properties around the village do not have something of Bert's work. He was the consummate craftsman - not a large man, but strong and capable of a range of heavy tasks. Everything he did was viewed as being of top quality and performed with the public interest always in mind.

It was not uncommon to see Bert at work perched on the church roof and invariably with a pipe in his mouth. People laughingly recall how he was inclined to catch himself alight from placing his un-extinguished pipe into a pocket, frequently requiring wife Jane to repair burnt clothing.

Bert (in the hat) on the job, somewhere in Minsterworth, with his uncle Charlie Prosser

As a young man he took part in the building of the Minsterworth Memorial (later Village) Hall and his experience and knowledge of that building was much valued by the hall's management committee (of which he was a life member for many years). He was also the main contractor for building work required on the parish church, just one of the services he contributed to the church on top of being Secretary of the Parochial Church Council, a sidesman and churchwarden. Bert also found time to be actively engaged on the local Parish Council. He was elected councillor in 1946 and served on the council until 1980, during which time for a period he acted as clerk and then for 27 years as chairman - the longest period in office served by the chairman in the history of the Parish Council. When almost 80, he was obliged to give up smoking for the sake of his health and to undergo surgery to remove part of a leg. This entailed having a false leg fitted. Despite continuous discomfort, this seems not to have affected Bert who (much to the alarm of wife Jane) continued to climb his ladders, remaining characteristically cheerful and fully involved in village life.

Bert Prosser, as a churchwarden of St Peter's church Minsterworth, makes a presentation to the vicar the Rev. Venables on the latter's retirement in 1972.

Bert also stood out in the community because of his abiding interest in the village generally, its history and natural environment - an interest honed over a lifetime spent in and around the place. One feels that he knew almost every square foot of the parish intimately. Quite late in life, he produced a comprehensive listing of all the ancient field names of the parish along with his own observations on their significance. He took special interest in the numerous commemorative trees that have been planted in the parish from as early as the coronation of Edward VII in 1902. We also have his own handwritten notes, evidently prepared for a comprehensive talk on the history of the village, the river, the church, the roads and the old ways of life which he remembered from being a boy (when playing marbles in the middle of the main road was accepted fun!). In fact, Bert loved reminiscing about things past. At gatherings, when he came out with the opener " I mind the time when …." or "when I was a boy ….", everyone knew they were about to receive a fascinating and usually relevant anecdote from the past. This was what the vicar, Canon Jenkins, may partly have had in mind when, at a PCC meeting in January 1988 soon after Bert's death, he paid tribute to Bert and his long service to the church, meaningfully adding:

> …. We shall miss his penetrating questions and reminiscences.

On his death, the church bells rang throughout the parish and a special service was held in the church.

In his life and work, Bert Prosser embodied service to the local community and a love of the country ways of life. His own life spanned almost a century of technological and social changes but he seems not to have been fazed by these, while also retaining the basic timeless skills of the creative country craftsman. At the end of that same interview that Bert Prosser had with the BBC's Stephen Wright, he was asked if he was still happy in Minsterworth. His reply was:

> Me? I'm bound to be ain't I. Ninety three and I ... where else can I go? My family have been here for hundreds of years. I'm the last; I'm the last………

Rest In Peace, Bert.

X.

BIBLIOGRAPHY AND AUTHOR'S ACKNOWLEDGEMENTS

I. Victorian Minsterworth
In putting together this article, use was made of a variety of documentary sources on Minsterworth held by the Glos. Archives (G.A.), as well as the draft volume of the *Victoria County History for Gloucestershire* covering Minsterworth which, although awaiting full publication, is already accessible on-line (www.victoriacountyhistory.ac.uk/counties/gloucestershire/work-in-progress/minsterworth). Where other published sources have been used, these are named in the text. Much additional information was derived from the manuscript daybook compiled by William Viner-Ellis covering the years 1824 to 1865. The author is grateful to Mrs Felicity Karger (a descendant of Mr Viner-Ellis) for making this intriguing material available for study. For anyone wishing to find out more regarding the union workhouse system, I can recommend the work of Peter Higginbotham available both in published form and on-line (www.user.ox.ac.uk/-peter/workhouse).

II. The House that Daniel Built
Numerous documentary sources in the Glos. Archives relating to the Ellis and Viner-Ellis families of Elmore and Mimsterworth and their estates (e.g. D1501, D640/T107, D3398 1/8) and various registers of landowners.
Aforementioned day book of William Viner-Ellis senior.
Aforementioned draft Victoria County History volume.

III. Just a Piece of Old Cloth.
The following published sources were used in the production of this article:
BAGNELL-OAKELEY M E, ' Ancient Church Embroidery in Gloucestershire' in *Transactions of the Bristol and Gloucestershire Archaeological Society* **11** (1886-87), pp.246-259.
BETTEY J H; *Suppression of the Monasteries in the West Country* (1989), Alan Sutton.
BROWNE A L; 'Richard Pate MP for Gloucester', *Transactions of the Bristol and Gloucestershire Archaeological Society* **56** *(1934), pp.201-225.*
BUCKLAND K; 'The Skenfrith Cope and Its Companions', *Textile History* **14** (2) (1983), pp.125-139.
DUFFY E; *The Stripping of the Altars: Traditional Religion in England, 1400-1580 (*1992) (Yale University Press.).
DUFFY E; *The Voices of Morebath: Reformation and Rebellion in an English village (*2001) (Yale University Press).
HERBERT N M (Ed.); 'City of Gloucester', *Victoria County History for Gloucestershire,* vol.4 (1988), pp.317-319.
POWELL K G; 'The Social Background to the Reformation in Gloucestershire', in *Transactions of the Bristol and Gloucestershire Archaeological Society* **92** *(1973),* pp.96-120.

POWELL K G and WILSON J; 'The Chipping Campden Altar Hangings' in *Transactions of the Bristol and Gloucestershire Archaeological Society* **115** (1997), pp.233-243.
1953 Cheltenham Art Gallery & Museum Exhibition Catalogue *The Royal Houses of Tudor and Stuart ,1485-1774.*
Hockaday Abstracts for Minsterworth Parish; GA 8/304/3.

The author is especially grateful to Ms Wendy Toulson ACR, Textile Conservator, for her most helpful advice on the subject of the Minsterworth embroidery. (wendytoulson.james@btinternet.com).

IV. Lamentable Happenings.
Sources as indicated in the text. Particularly valuable were parish records for Minsterworth and Elmore parishes and oral history material obtained by the author from past residents of Minsterworth, notably Mrs Cristobel Mortimer, Mrs Felicity Karger and Mr John Browning, to whom many thanks are due .

V. Hellfire Jack.
The author has been greatly helped by a number of local folk who remember Charlie Trigg and followed his fortunes over time. Deserving of particular mention are Mr and Mrs Arthur Jayne of The Whitehouse Minsterworth and Mrs Joan Gardner of Birdwood, all of whom have links with the Greening/Trigg families. Mr Keith Pearson, Charlie's grandson now living in the United States and who has done a great deal of research into his grandfather, also provided much valuable information for this article.

VI. Why Should the Devil have all the Good Tunes?
Oxford Dictionary of National Biography
The Journal of the Reverend John Wesley, vol. II (1829), p.356.
The Works of the Rev. John Wesley MA, vol. XVIII (1773).
Victoria County History for Gloucestershire, vol. 4 (1988), pp.319-334.
Centenary Handbook, Wesley Church , St George's Street, Cheltenham (1939).
MOSS P, *Historic Gloucester* (1993), pp.18-19.
SAWYER J, *The Story of Gloucestershire* (1907).
Various documents in Glos. Archives. relating to the registration of Dissenting Meeting Places in Gloucestershire.
The author is indebted also to information passed to him by Mr Walter Hurcombe, whose family were once closely connected with the Methodist Chapel at Minsterworth.

VII. Going, Going, Gone.
DAVIES G, 'The Old Road from Over to Minsterworth', *Glevensis 12 (1978), p.*10.
DRAPER S, *Victoria County History for Gloucestershire, vol. 13,* as yet unpublished but accessible on-line (see above).

Ecclesiastical Commissioners' Files relating to St. Peter's, Minsterworth; ref. ECE/7/1/27816/1-3
GWATKIN G, 1839 Tithe Map of Minsterworth (1993).
Terrier of the Freehold and Leasehold Estates of Charles Barrow Esq. Together with the Free-lands intermixed In the Parish and Manor of Minsterworth In the County of Gloucester; by Ferdinando Stratford, Engineer, 1757. Glos. Archives PA218/3.
JOHNSON M, 'The Street at Minsterworth and the Road from Over', *Glevensis 29 (1996), pp.*39-44.
MOORE-SCOTT T, *Medieval Fish Weirs on the mid-tidal reaches of the River Severn (Ashleworth-Arlingham),* Glevensis 42 (2009), pp.31-44.
WATERS B, *Severn Tide* (1947), esp. p.56.
YOUNG A, *A Six Weeks Tour through the southern counties of England and Wales*, London (1768), pp.141-144.

VIII. Literary Links
Walter Map:
The original of *De Nugis Curialium* is held by the Bodleian Library in Oxford but translations of it have been published in several sources including: *The Cymmrodorian Record Series no.IX (1923)* (English only - a copy is in Gloucester Shire Hall Library) and in *Clarendon Press (1914 edition)* (PRO library ref 941.031) (Latin and English).
BROOKE C N L, 'Map, Walter (*d.* 1209/10)', *Oxford Dictionary of National Biography*, Oxford University Press, 2004.
FINBERG H P R, *Early Charters of the West Midlands.* Leicester. (1961), p.145.
John Gwillim:
Oxford Dictionary of National Biography.
Oxford Univ. Reg. (Oxf. History Society), vol ii, pt. ii, p.98.
Glos. Archives, esp. D640/T92 and T93 (the latter including four documents carrying the great wax seal of 'John Gwillim of Minsterworth'.
Hockaday Abstracts for Minsterworth.
Conan Doyle:
Oxford Dictionary of National Biography.
Richard Lancelyn Green; *Louise Hawkins and her Family,* date unknown (written for the Sherlock Holmes Society of London).
Gloucester Citizen, November 20th 1991.
Gloucestershire Archives: various documentary sources relating to the Hawkins family of Minsterworth.
F W Harvey:
Oxford Dictionary of National Biography.
BODEN A and THORNTON R K R (Eds.), *F.W. Harvey, Selected Poems*; Douglas McLean Publishing (2011).
PILBEAM A, *Viewing Gloucestershire: Gloucestershire through the Eyes of its Authors;* Nonsuch, 2006.
Personal communications between the author and the late Patrick Harvey, son of F W Harvey.

H G Wells:
Oxford Dictionary of National Biography.
WELLS H G, *An Experiment in Autobiography, Discoveries and Conclusion of a Very Ordinary Brain (since 1866),* (1934). (ebooks.adelaide.edu/wells/hg).
BBC Radio Times, feature on *War of the Worlds by Jon Manchip White*; (www.war-of the-worlds.co.uk/war_of_the_worlds_bbc_1950_article.htm.).
The author is grateful for valuable information received from Myk Davis of the H G Wells Society (in New Zealand) and also to Ms Nickie Milligan of Minsterworth, who first drew attention to the village's connection with H G Wells.

Jon Manchip White:
Biographical detail provided on-line by Iris Books Inc. (Manchip White's American publishers) (www.irisbooks.com/manchip%20white); a second on-line source, www.enotes.com/topic/Jon_Manchip_White, provided useful information on Manchip White's published works and filmography.
Registers of Electoral Rolls for Minsterworth, 1959-1964; Glos. Archives ref. Q/RER West Glos.

IX. 'A Good All Round Man'

This piece on Bert Prosser could not have been written without the help of numerous individuals, each with their own memories of him. Especially helpful have been Mrs Sue Barnett and Mrs Ann Alford (Bert's daughter and niece respectively) who provided valuable detail about Bert's life. Valuable background was also provided by Mr William Mogg of Minsterworth who in his youth spent a number of years working with and for Bill.

The punt made by Bill Prosser of Minsterworth is currently held in store at the National Maritime Museum (NMM) Cornwall, on loan from NMM Greenwich, where all the details are kept (reference BAE0067).

Finally, the author expresses special thanks to Anthony Boden and Eric Miller for their editorial assistance and, of course, to his wife, Ruth, whose interest and support were a mainstay throughout this project.

INDEX OF CONTENTS

A

Abergavenny	32
Adelaide	50
Andrew St (Westminster) (dedication)	51
Appithorne (house)	54, 78, 79
Appletree Inn	12, 75, 88
Arlingham	42
Assundun, battle of	82
Aston, M	70
Augustine, St (abbey) – see Bristol	
Aust	60
Austen, Jane	81
Austria	50
Averidge (field)	18, 19, 23

B

Badgeworth	18
'Baedeker' (air raids)	47
Bagnell-Oakley, Mary Ellen	40
Baldock Field (Herts)	61
Balfour Rev.	17
Baptist, movement	57
Barrett, William	22
Barrow, Sir Charles	18, 44
Bartlett, Canon	38, 40
Bath	47, 81
Bayeux tapestry	29
B.B.C.	94
Beachley	60
Beckenham (Kent)	99
Bellringing	8, 98, 104
Berkeley	32
Castle papers	42
Bird In Hand (inn)	8
See also Severn Bore (inn)	
Birdwood	45, 51
Black Drive	44
Boden, Anthony	88
Bodnams (house)	55, 77, 97
Boevey, Catherine	59
Boyce (family)	9
Annie	9
Amelia	9
Elsie	65
Fred	43, 44
Harold	43, 44
Brasenose, college (Oxford)	84
Brecon	60
Bridgewater	70
Brighton	51
Brockwell, Rev C A B	41
Bristol	60, 77, 102
St Augustine's, abbey	35
British Museum	94
Broadoak	90
Bromley (Kent)	92
Brown, Thomas	4

B (cont)

Browning (family)	44, 45
John	44, 45, 80
Bruegel, Peter (artist)	34
Bryson, Bill	46
Bulley	24
Bullock, George	24
Burke, Thomas	15
Bury Lane	76
Butt (family)	13, 65

C

Calcotts Green	6, 7, 12, 43, 44, 56, 63, 64, 65, 68, 74, 77
Cambridge	93
Canterbury	47, 81
Chamberlayne, John (Jack)	28
Chantry (-ies)	3, 34, 36, 39
Chapel (see also Wesleyan Chapel)	5, 10
Cottage	57, 64-66, 87
House	65
Road	65
Cardiff	93
Catterick Bridge	50
Charities	6
Chasuble	30, 33, 38, 39
Chaucer	81
Chaxhill	50
Cheltenham (Spa)	9, 39, 62
Art Gallery & Museum	38, 40
Chepstow	73
Child, Mr	65
Church	3
Landing Yard	69
of England	6, 57, 62
non-conformist	5
St Peter's, Minsterworth	8, 10. 26, 29, 38, 41, 42, 43, 44, 47, 54, 67, 75, 79, 98, 99, 103
Volunteer Training Corps	27
Churchdown	63
Churcham	23, 28, 46, 74, 75, 76
Lane	76
Ci(y)der	14, 17, 43
Cirencester	
Abbey	39
Clement, St (dedication)	33
Clifford, Richard	63
Cnut, King	82
Climperland (field)	13
Cobbett, William	2, 3
Colchester –Wemyss (family)	9
Coldwell, Dennis	67
Coleford	60, 61
Coleridge, Mr Justice	53

C (cont)

Conan Doyle, Sir Arthur	85, 86, 87
Alleyne	86
Louisa (see also Hawkins)	85, 86, 87
Mary	86, 87
Congregational Church	57
Cope	33, 38, 39, 41
Copper King (race horse)	50
Cornham	34, 71, 75
Corn Laws	14
Cotswold Countryside Museum	101
Cowley, John	36
Cranham	90
Crawley-Boevey (family)	9
Cray Croft	27, 45
Cromwell, Thomas	35
Crump	
Susannah	6, 18, 19
William	18
Crypt School, see Gloucester	
Cyprus Cottage	50

D

Dalmatic	30
Daniels, Oliver (Moreton Valence)	98
Davis, Lawrence (Tibberton)	11
Deerhurst, priory	39
Denny	8, 71
Rock	71
Bridge	78
Dennys (family)	84
Dexter, Colin	81
Dinny	50
Disney, Walt	94
Dissenters	57, 58, 63
Duchy of Lancaster	70
Dulwich	51
Duni	12, 13, 14, 18, 20, 69, 77, 78, 83, 100
Farm	14, 17, 19, 25, 28
House	3, 4, 6, 14, 19, 21, 22, 23, 27, 28
Villa	97

E

Eamehill	65
Ecclesiastical Commissioners	79
Edinburgh	50, 86
University Medical School	86
Edmund Ironside, King	82, 83
Edward VI, King	35, 36, 37
Edward VII, Kng	104
Elizabeth I, Queen	32, 37
Elizabeth II, Queen	38
Ellis (family) (see also Viner-Ellis)	8, 13, 17
Ann(e)	8, 23
Daniel	18, 19, 20, 21, 28
Mary	19
William	21, 25
the Misses	24
Elm(s) Farm	2, 56, 80, 92
Elmore	18, 42, 97
Elmore Back	8, 13, 42, 71, 72
Enclosure (of fields)	13

E (cont)

Epney	21
Epsom (races)	50
Epworth (Lincs)	58
Evans (family)	3
Charity	6
Hector, police constable	44
Exeter	47, 48

F

Farm Café	78
Ferry	71, 72
Cottage	77
Fielden, Mrs	27
Fishery(ies)	21, 24
Fishing	15, 70, 71, 98
Fishmonger	21
Fish weirs	70, 71
Flat, The	8
Flaxley	9
Abbey	32, 59
Flooding	42, 43, 44, 75
Football Club	11, 98, 99
Forest of Dean	78, 83, 91
Foreign Office	94
Forge, The (Minsterworth)	96, 97, 99, 101, 102
Framilode	21
Frampton	42
France	40, 50
Francis, Joan (Jane)	99
Frenzy (race horse)	50

G

Gambier-Parry (family)	9
Gardner, Joan	51
Geoffrey of Monmouth	81
George, St (dedication)	33, 36
Georgia (USA)	58
Germany	58
Gibbs, J Arthur	3
Glastonbury	82
Gloucester	4, 11, 15, 16, 18, 24, 32, 37, 42, 54, 60, 62, 63, 69, 70, 73, 74, 75
Abbey/Cathedral	24, 35, 36, 38, 39, 40, 58, 81
Alderman (of)	23
Assizes	60
Bell Inn	58
Bishop of	63
Boothall	59
City Congregation	58
Cobblers' Hall	59
College of Technology	98
Congregational church	24
Crypt school	6, 7, 21, 58, 98
Denmark Road School	54
Election Commission	24
Fire Brigade	44
Folk Museum	101
General Hospital	55
Infirmary	6, 22
Jail	36
Journal	6, 10, 40, 44, 45, 60, 63

G (cont)

Kimbrose Triangle	59
Mayor (of)	23, 58
Northgate Street, Lower	59
Royal centre	83
Southgate Street	58
Tollbooth	59
St Bartholomew's Hospital	59
St John's Lane	88
St Oswald's priory	35
St Peter's Catholic church	24
West Bridge	36
Worcester Street	59
Gloucester – Sharpness Canal	69
Gloucestershire Regiment	89
Gobey, Cheryl	9
Godfrey, Fred (songwriter)	49
Goodman, Richard (surveyor, Lydney)	19, 20, 21
Graingers (house)	77
Grange, The (hotel)	28
Great Exhibition, The	2
Great War, The	17
Greenacres (house)	78
Greening (family)	51, 54
Caroline	50
Derrick	51
Mary	54
William	50
Griggs W (jockey)	51, 52
Guilds (ecclesiastic)	36
Gurney, Ivor	88
Gwillim, Sir John (herald)	83, 84, 85
John senior	83

H

Hailes Abbey	2, 39
Ham Green	73
Hampton	18, 76
Hartpury	63, 88
Harvey (family)	
Anne	90
Bernard	88
Eileen	90
Eric	88
F. W. (poet)	72, 88-91, 102
Gladys	88
Howard	88
Matilda	88
Patrick	88, 90
Hatfield (Herts)	61
Hatheways (manor of)	83
Hawkins (family)	3, 6, 13
Emily	85
Jack	85
Jeremiah	85
Louisa ('Touie')	85
Mary	63
Hayward (family)	
John, Joan and Thomas	46
Healey C & Sons (Gloucester)	98
Henry II, King	81
Henry VII, King	32
Henry VIII, King	32, 34, 35, 71

H (cont)

Hereford	84
Bishop of	81
Diocese of	81, 82
Heyward, Nicholas	38
High Leadon, Court	23
Highcross	12, 73, 74, 75
Highlay (house)	80, 87
Highnam	9, 11, 46, 74, 75
Cricket Club	98, 99
roundabout	12
High View (house)	91
Hindhead (Surrey)	87
Hobart	50
'Holy Club'	58
Home Orchard (house)	78
Holy Cross, The (dedication)	33
Hooper, John, Bishop	37
Hoper, Richard	38
Howells, Herbert	88
Hucclecote	63
Huntingdon, Countess of	59
Hurcombe (family)	64
Walter	64
Hyet, Elizabeth	38
Hyett, Charity	6

I

Icknield	82
Innocent IV, Pope	30
Ireland	50

J

Jayne (family)	
Marion	91
Roger	54
Jenkins, Canon	104
Jubilee (Queen Victoria)	16, 17

K

Karger, Felicity	22, 26
Katharine, St (dedication)	33
Katherine of Aragon, queen	32, 35, 36
Kempe, Sibble	46
Kermesse	34
Keylocke, John	38
King's Head (alehouse)	8
Kippax, Walter	53
Kynge, William	83

L

Laken, Tony	66
Lamp Half Acre (field)	34
Lane, Margery	54
Laurie Lee	81
Leckhampton	85
Leckie, Jean Blythe	87
Leicester, Bishops of	81
Linton, Lower	73, 74

L (cont)

'Little Minsterworth'	13
Littledean	32
Littles (field)	63
Littleton, William	17, 25
London	16, 24, 29, 47, 51, 82, 85, 86, 93, 94
Bishops of	81
Normal School	92
Royal College of Sciences	92
University College	23
V & A Museum	40
Longbrook	13, 14, 76
Lower Moorcroft (farm)	12, 85, 87
Lowestoft	53
Lubeck	47
Lydney	19, 91
Lymington (Hants)	25
Lyn Paddock	44, 78

M

Manchip White (family)	
Bronwen	94
Jon	93-95
Rhiannon	94
Valerie	93
Manton (racing stables)	50
Map, Walter	81-83
Mary (Queen of Scotland)	36
Mary, St (dedication)	34
Mary, The Virgin (dedication)	33
Matilda, Queen	25
Matson	39
May Hill	11
Maynard, Douglas	54
Maynard Davis, Winifred Rhoda	51
Mee, Arthur	41
Meekins (house)	97, 99
Mendelssohn	62
Messenger, Mary	65
Methodist(s)	58, 60, 62
Chapel	77
Movement	57, 59, 61
Mill(s)	78, 79
Minchinhampton	60
Minsterworth	
Court	23, 25, 26, 27, 28, 45, 83, 93, 94
Family (medieval)	33
Forge	96
Ham	42
Horticultural Show	26
House	19
Memorial Hall	26
Parish Council	103
Parochial Church Council	103, 104
School	6, 7, 12, 13, 26, 71, 94
Scouts	63
Vicarage	11, 12, 76, 79
Village Hall	26, 99, 103
Mogg (family)	65
Charlie	65
Monmouth	32, 85
Moorcote	83

M (cont)

Moorcottes Lane	74
Moreton Valence	98
Mortimer, Christabel	43
Murcott	12, 13
Farm	23
Murrell's End	88

N

Naight, The	9, 16, 45, 63, 80
National Maritime Museum	97
Negus, Arthur	28
Nettleship, Rev Arthur	79, 80
Newbury	50
Newent	44
Newnham	11, 15, 73, 75
Parish church	81
Pound	11, 78
Newport	40, 70
Nicholas, St (dedication)	33
Non-conformists	57
North America	58
Norwich	47

O

Oakle	
House	65
Street	8, 26, 65, 75, 77, 100
Odo, Bishop	29
Old Chapel House	63, 64, 65
Old Passage	60
Old Road House	80
Oppithorne (field)	13
Oprirs, Mary	4
'Opus Anglicanum'	29, 30
Orchard End	9
Outram, The Misses	28
Over	63, 73, 74
Oxford	24, 58, 61, 81
Lincoln College	58

P

Painswick	60
Paris	81
Parish Rate	13
Parlour Farm	12
Pate, Sir Richard	39, 40
Paul, St	31
Pearson (family)	
Keith	52, 53
Rev Peter	54, 55
Rachel	54
Pershbrook	14
Cottage	72, 77
Phelps (family)	
Arthur	41
Fanny	78
'Granny'	44
Pill	60
Pins (manufacture of)	4

P (cont)

Plackett Pool	21, 28
Orchard	23
Police	
Special Constabulary	99
station	78
Poleyard	97, 100
Pool End Cottage	44, 45, 80
Poor,	
Guardians of	22
Law	4, 6
Rate	4
Population (of Minsterworth)	13
Portsmouth	86
Pound	12, 77
Cottage	12, 77, 80
Lane	75, 77, 80
Preen, William	63
Presbyterian movement	57
Pretty Polly (race horse)	50, 51
Price, Mr	24
Prosser (family)	
Albert George (Bert)	55, 70, 72, 96-105
Charlie	102
George	96
Jane	103, 104
Jim	96, 102
Lucy	96
Susan	99
William	97, 98
Prosser's Forge	78, 97
Yard	70, 97
Pump Court	12, 76
Puritan movement	57
Purton	60

Q

R

Raglan, castle	32
Raikes, Robert	6, 58
Railway (to S Wales)	13
Raine, Rev James	25
Margaret Hannah	25
Raleigh, Sir Walter	37
Redlands	12, 88, 89, 90
Reformation	30, 31, 33, 35, 37, 40
Richmond	87
Roads (see also Turnpike)	11, 12, 15, 69, 71, 72-74
Robinswood	64
Rodley	21
Rosedale (house)	12, 78, 100
Rosedrop (race horse)	50
Ross-on-Wye	11, 82
Rothschild (family)	50, 53
Rowbotham, Fred	101
Royal Agricultural Society	26
Royal College of Arms	83, 84
Royal School of Needlework	40
Ryders (house)	80

S

Salmon Inn	8, 71
Sandown Park (race course)	50
School Alley	6
Selwyn (family)	47
Severn River	11, 15, 24, 32, 42, 43, 56, 69, 70, 71, 73, 91
Bank (house)	3, 12, 21, 22, 23, 27, 28
Bore (inn)	8
estuary	42
Severn River Board	101
Shadbridge	76
Meadow (field)	76
Shakespeare	81
Ship Inn	45
Silent Whistle (inn)	8
Siston	84
Slad	81
Slag block	77
Smart, Ernest Wallace	41
Snowdrop Cottage	44
Somerset	43
South Norwood	86, 87
Southsea	85
Speed, John	85
Staite, Joanne	65
Stamford (Lincs)	61
Stanilade (field)	71
Stephens (family)	64, 67, 77
Annie	65
John Clifford	16, 65
Martha	67
Mary	65
Richard	63, 67
Stone Yard Cottage(s)	96, 97
Stratford-on-Avon	81
Street, The	56, 63, 65, 66, 75, 79
Street End Cottage	43, 44, 75
Sunday School(s)	6, 58, 63, 65
Swindon	90
Switzerland	50, 53
Sym(e)s (family)	3
William	80

T

Taterbury Cottage	9
Taynton	23
Tenesse University of	94
Texas, University of	74
Thomas St (dedication)	33
Three Choirs Festival	9
Thornton-in-Lonsdale (Lancs)	86
Thursby, George (jockey)	51
Tibberton	11
Times, The	53, 55
Tithe Cottage	23, 27, 76
Tovey, Ann	46
Traveller, Benjamin	16
Trigg (family)	54
Alice	51
Catherine	55
Ellen	50
Phyllis	51, 53, 54, 55

T (cont)

    Rhoda   50
    William   50
    Winifred   52, 53
Treasure, Frank (solicitor)   88
Tuffeyhayes   43
Turnpike
    Gloucester to Newnham   11, 15, 16
Twickenham   87

U

Unitarian Church   57
United States   54
Upper Moorcroft   13, 73, 74
Usk   32

V

Vatican   29, 30
Vicarage   12
Venables, Rev   104
Victoria, Queeen   2, 5, 7, 16
Viner, Mary   18
Viner-Brady, family   28
    Annabel   47, 48
    Jennifer   47, 48
    Molly   48
    Noel   28
Viner-Ellis (family)   3, 19, 22, 26, 28, 44, 97
    Edmund   23, 24, 25
    Elizabeth   23
    George   23, 24, 25
    Godfrey William   25, 26, 28
    Morwenna (Armstrong)   26
    Primrose (Armstrong)   26
    William (senior)   4, 6, 7, 9, 14, 15, 16, 17, 24, 63
    William (junior)   23, 24
Viner Vyner Ellis (family)
    Margaret Hannah   26-28, 65, 66
    Margery   25, 45
    William   25
Vining, Mary   28

W

Watery Lane   75
Walmore Hill   50
Waters, Brian   70
Watham, Sam   70
Watkins, Eric   56, 80
Webb, 'Granny'   44
Weir House   87
Wells (family)
    Charles   92
    Joseph   92
Wells, H G (writer)   92 - 93
Wesley
    Charles   58, 61
    John   58 - 61
Wesleyan Chapel   6, 7, 56, 65
Wesleyan Methodist Conference   62

W (cont)

Wesleyan Methodist Society   63, 66
Westbury-on-Severn   4, 9, 23, 24, 46, 81- 83
    Chapel   62
    Workhouse   4
Whitefield, George   58–60, 62
White House, The   50, 51, 54-55
William, The Conqueror   29
Williams, Billy (entertainer)   49
Winchcombe   1, 32, 38, 39, 40
    St Peter's abbey   31
Windmill   79
    Acre (field)   78
    Bush Piece (field)   78
    Hill (field)   78
    Piece (field)   78
Windsor Castle   93
Wintle Charity   6
Witts, Rev F E   11
Wright, Stephen (BBC Glos)   96, 105

X

Y

York   47
Young, Arthur   4, 11, 15, 73

Z

Zurich Insurance Co   98